J949.4 LEVY
Levy, Patricia,
Switzerland /

CULTURES OF THE WORLD
Switzerland

Cavendish
Square

New York

Published in 2016 by Cavendish Square Publishing, LLC
243 5th Avenue, Suite 136, New York, NY 10016
Copyright © 2016 by Cavendish Square Publishing, LLC

Third Edition

This publication represents the opinions and views of the author based on his or her personal experience, knowledge, and research. The information in this book serves as a general guide only. The author and publisher have used their best efforts in preparing this book and disclaim liability rising directly or indirectly from the use and application of this book.
CPSIA Compliance Information: Batch #WS15CSQ
All websites were available and accurate when this book was sent to press.

Cataloging-in-Publication Data

Levy, Patricia.
Switzerland / by Patricia Levy, Richard Lord, and Debbie Nevins.
p. cm. — (Cultures of the world)
Includes index.
ISBN 978-1-50260-344-9 (hardcover) ISBN 978-1-50260-345-6 (ebook)
1. Switzerland — Juvenile literature. I. Levy, Patricia, 1951-. II. Title.
DQ17.L48 2016
949.4—d23

Writers, Patricia Levy, Richard Lord; Debbie Nevins, third edition
Editorial Director, third edition: David McNamara
Editor, third edition: Debbie Nevins
Art Director, third edition: Jeffrey Talbot
Designer, third edition: Jessica Nevins
Production Manager, third edition: Jennifer Ryder-Talbot
Cover Picture Researcher: Stephanie Flecha
Picture Researcher, third edition: Jessica Nevins

PICTURE CREDITS

PRECEDING PAGE
Two Swiss musicians play the alpenhorn.

Printed in the United States of America

CONTENTS

SWITZERLAND TODAY

ARE THE SWISS THE HAPPIEST PEOPLE ON EARTH? YOU MIGHT not think such a thing could be measured, since there are happy people and miserable people everywhere. However, yes, it is possible to determine the relative happiness of a people according to nationality. And yes, the Swiss stand blissfully at the very top of the world in terms of "life satisfaction." That is one of the eleven categories in the 2015 Better Life Index, a scorecard of thirty-four nations' well-being published by the Organization for Economic Cooperation and Development (OECD). The other ten categories are housing, income, jobs, community, education, environment, civic engagement, health, safety, and work-life balance.

When all eleven factors are weighted evenly, Switzerland comes out sixth. It gets pulled out of top place by its very low score in the civic engagement category. There, it falls into the bottom 20 percent of the OECD's nations. That anomaly makes sense, however, when you understand Switzerland's special political and governmental organization, which is unlike any other on Earth.

The OECD index is only one measure of a country's standing. There are others, and Switzerland comes out among the top few in all of them. In the 2014 Legatum

At the 1920 International Feminist Convention in Geneva, women campaigned for the right to vote. In Switzerland, they would have to wait several more decades.

Prosperity Index, which ranks 142 countries according to wealth, economic growth, and quality of life, Switzerland is number two, after Norway. In the 2013 World Happiness Report, published by United Nations' Sustainable Development Solutions Network, Switzerland snagged the number three spot, after Denmark and Norway. According to the World Economic Forum's 2013 Human Capital Report, Switzerland invests more in the health, education, and talent of its people than any other country in the world.

None of this is to say that Switzerland has no problems. Of course it does. But in the global scheme of things, this small but mightily important country is doing very well indeed.

Switzerland is a country in Western Europe that breaks rules and turns many assumptions upside down. It is a landlocked nation—it has no seacoast—but yet it has plentiful water resources. Within its relatively small area, its people speak four national languages, none of which are English, and three of those are official languages. There is no one tongue that all Swiss speak, and the country's cultural and linguistic populations are clustered in separate regions. That alone would seem to indicate a lack of cohesiveness leading to national insecurity—and yet, the country is quite solid and has been for a long time. It is a progressive, forward looking, fair-minded country, and yet Swiss women didn't have full suffrage—the right to vote—in all regions until 1990!

Switzerland is largely mountainous, secluded, and lacks natural resources, and yet its economy is strong. It's a major player on the international marketplace. Switzerland values its neutrality, yet has a high-tech, highly armed citizen army into which all male citizens are drafted. Its industries range from technology to textiles to tourism; its weather ranges from areas of year-long snow to Mediterranean heat.

Significantly, Switzerland is in the very heart of Europe, but refuses to join the European Union (EU). The Swiss are famously independent, as evidenced by their historic neutrality. They have so far resisted joining the EU even as that decision threatens to hurt their economy and relations with the rest of Europe.

Not least, Switzerland is a land of spectacular natural beauty, which attracts high numbers of tourists. Many people have an image of Switzerland as charming and quaint. They imagine pastoral scenes of simple people living the good life against backdrops of breathtaking mountain scenery. That good Swiss life, in this fantasy, involves happy people living in pretty chalets, wearing colorfully embroidered peasant clothing, yodeling into the alpine distances, making cheese and chocolate, eating fondue, and crafting world-class watches while adorable cuckoo clocks announce the time.

This vision of Switzerland is true in its parts, but it's hardly the full picture. Consider a similar fantasy of the United States, in which everyone is a movie star or rock star, plays baseball or football, eats hamburgers and Mom's apple pie, and wears cowboy hats and boots. On any given detail, the stereotype says "American," but as a generalization, it's flat, one-dimensional, misleading, and a bit dated. So it is with the Swiss stereotype.

Switzerland is a very advanced, twenty-first century country, full of complexity and contradictions. It's a wealthy country and obviously a very successful one on many levels. All of that counts for a lot, because Switzerland today is undergoing changes. The Swiss, in general, do not like change. The Swiss are often described as somewhat bland, conservative people. They like the way things are in their country—who could blame them?—and don't see any need to change.

A tourist photo stop on Rigi Mountain ironically reinforces the stereotypical image of Switzerland.

A vivid example of this attitude can be seen in its recent move to limit immigration. Switzerland hosts an unusually large number of foreigners. In 2015, foreign nationals made up 23.5 percent of the population, with about 80,000 people immigrating each year. Another 230,000 cross the border daily for work. The Swiss need highly qualified people in their chemical, pharmaceutical, and biotech industries to help keep those businesses globally competitive.

However, in 2014, the right-wing Swiss People's Party proposed an initiative aimed at limiting immigration through quotas. It passed by a slender majority of 50.3 percent of the vote. Some people believe the vote was prompted by a fear of Muslim immigrants, particularly those who hold fundamentalist beliefs. Muslims make up about 5 percent of Switzerland's eight million people. The Constitution upholds freedom of religion, but the voters' concerns seem to have more to do with Islam's potential impact on the Swiss way of life. One immigrant group in Bern, for example, in 2011 reportedly called for the white cross to be removed from the Swiss flag.

Demonstrators hold a banner in French which reads (in full, beyond the photo borders) "Together against exclusion and xenophobia, Swiss, immigrants, refugees, let us unite!"

The group suggested replacing it with a secular icon that doesn't favor or offend any religion, and which more accurately reflects Switzerland's multicultural reality. Following the 2015 attack on a Parisian magazine staff by Islamist terrorists, Swiss calls to curb Muslim immigration only rose higher.

The Swiss National Bank in Bern is the central bank of Switzerland.

While Switzerland grapples with its vision for its future, it is also being forced to confront some dark realities from its past. Its neutral role in World War II is being reevaluated. Many Swiss fervently believe that their spirited defense is what kept Nazi Germany from invading their small country, while Germany conquered much larger nations around it. Historical perspective suggests otherwise, and Switzerland today is compelled to confront some uncomfortable truths. This topic is discussed in more detail in this book.

Similarly, the country is being forced to change its nearly century-old tradition of bank secrecy. Switzerland is a giant in the international banking industry, and built its reputation on complete privacy for its clients. Tax evaders and other criminals found this practice very helpful and, as a result, hid ill-begotten fortunes in Swiss banks. Now, under pressure from the United States and the EU, the Swiss are being compelled to change their laws to conform to certain standards of transparency. This move will no doubt have a huge impact on their economy.

Switzerland today must decide where it fits in Europe, and in the world. The Swiss treasure their independent, isolationist, special status. But they also know they need to be part of the world beyond their mountain fortress. What does it mean to be Swiss in the twenty-first century? We know it's not a matter of yodeling and cuckoo clocks. The Swiss will decide the answers to these questions, and indications look very promising that they will find the right answers for their country's future. Welcome to Switzerland!

GEOGRAPHY

The Matterhorn, the most famous peak in Switzerland, rises over a small chalet on a green mountainside.

1

WHEN MOST PEOPLE THINK OF the landscape of Switzerland, they probably think of glacier-topped mountains and deep green valleys. Perhaps, if they are familiar with the story of Heidi, they imagine hillsides dotted with goats. They might picture cows in a high meadow, lazily grazing to the clang of bells on their necks. Those visions of Switzerland are true enough, but there is more to Switzerland than that. Large cosmopolitan cities are also part of the Swiss landscape, as are congested highways, and even, in a small section of Ticino, near the Italian border, palm trees.

Like its neighbor Austria, Switzerland is a landlocked country. It is bordered on the west by France, on the north by Germany, on the east by Austria and the tiny principality of Liechtenstein, and on the south by Italy. Switzerland is one of the smallest countries in Europe, both in terms of area and population. Covering 15,938 square miles (41,290 square kilometers), it has a population of only about eight million, of which some 20 percent are non-Swiss resident immigrants. However, Switzerland's position at the center of Europe makes it a significant

Switzerland has more than 1,500 lakes. At any point in the country, you are never more than 10 miles (16 kilometers) from a lake.

A meadow of crocus in an Alpine valley gleams before a spring storm.

country. To the northwest of the country is the Jura mountain range, while to the southeast are the Swiss Alps. Between the two mountain ranges lies the Mittelland, the hub of the country where the bulk of the population lives.

THE ALPS

The Alps are a crescent-shaped range of mountains beginning in southeastern France and extending across southern Switzerland into Austria. They are the largest mountain range in Europe. Three-fifths of Switzerland's landmass is covered by the Alps, but fewer than one-fifth of its people live there.

The Alps were formed in two stages millions of years ago. First, a period of mountain-building thrust up great arches of rock that buckled over and created the distinctive rock formations still visible today. A second episode of mountain-building pushed the whole chain even higher. Millions of years of erosion, followed by excavation by the great glaciers of the last Ice Age, created the complex shapes of today's Alps. The peaks of the Alps stood above

GREAT WALLS OF SNOW

When big masses of snow have their foundations loosened by rain or melted by warm winds, they roll down mountainsides. These incidents are known as avalanches. Tremors caused by loud noises can also cause avalanches.

Avalanches are most likely to occur when the gradient or slope of the mountainside is more than 22 degrees. An avalanche can reach speeds of up to 245 miles per hour (394 km per hour). The air pushed along in front of the avalanche can cause as much damage as the avalanche itself, which may destroy buildings or even bury towns. Due to the size of an avalanche and the speed at which it travels, it is impossible to stop or alter its course.

Every year brings tragedies in the mountains. On January 31, 2015, eight people died in four separate avalanches in one day in Switzerland. Then, three weeks later, another three were killed and two more were injured while skiing in an area called Death Valley in the Swiss Alps. Those incidents raised the death toll from avalanches in the Swiss Alps that winter to twenty-four.

The Swiss Institute for Snow and Avalanche Research conducts studies and gives warnings about avalanches. Since World War II, the organization has produced reports on snow conditions during the winter months to warn snow skiers and mountain climbers of possible avalanches. The Institute uses a five-level warning system to rate snow conditions and the possibility of avalanches, from low to very high.

In addition, Switzerland has terrestrial and air mountain rescue teams that are on call twenty-four hours a day. Many artificial structures have also been built along the most susceptible stretches of roads and around Alpine villages to hold back the snow slides.

the glaciers and were unaffected by them, but the glaciers filled the whole Mittelland region. Other glaciers carved out the valleys of the Alps. Where the glaciers finally disappeared, they left behind great mounds of debris that blocked the rivers and created the beautiful lakes of Switzerland.

Today the Alps contain more than a thousand glaciers that are still at work carving out ever-deeper valleys. Compared to the great glaciers of the last Ice Age, however, these are tiny. The largest of them is the Aletsch Glacier, which is 14.3 miles (23 km) long and located near Bern.

The Alps are the source of many of Europe's major rivers. The high mountains with sharp inclines and the bountiful supply of water give Switzerland one of its greatest natural assets—hydroelectric power. The upper valleys of two rivers, the Rhine and the Rhône, divide the Alps into a northern and southern range of mountains. The appearance of the mountains varies according to the height and degree of exposure to winds. Up to 4,920 feet (1,500 meters) in elevation, the land is used for agriculture. Above this are coniferous forests. Above the tree line, the mountain pastures begin.

A young woman hikes above the Aletsch Glacier.

Beyond 9,840 feet (3,000 m) high, little can grow, except a few mosses and lichens that cling to the bare rocks. The highest point in Switzerland is the Dufourspitze at 15,204 feet (4,637 m). The Matterhorn, with its distinctive outline, is slightly lower at 14,692 feet (4,481 m).

THE JURA

The Jura (YOOR-ah) region covers 225 miles (362 km) of the French-Swiss border. The highest point of this mountain range is Crêt de la Neige (Mount Neige) in France, at 5,636 feet (1,718 m).

The rocky peaks of the Jura Mountains extend into the distance.

Jura is a Celtic word that means "forest." The mountain range was formed by the same massive earth movements that built the Alps over a long period of time. These upheavals, whose effects impacted all of Europe and beyond, were caused when the continents of Europe and Africa collided. The Jura are lower than the Alps. While the Alps are made up of a large variety of materials, the Jura mountains are more consistent and are made up of sandstone, limestone, and marl. They also contain many fossils, which tell us that a long time ago these mountains lay beneath a shallow sea. In fact, this mountain range gives its name to a period of geological time—the Jurassic. The fossils found in the Jura are the remains of creatures from the Jurassic period.

While the peaks of the Alps escaped the rounding and weathering effects of the Ice Age, the Jura, being much lower, did not. Therefore they are characteristically rounded in shape. The tops of the mountains are sparsely forested because they are above the tree line, but the valleys are wooded. Plateaus created by the erosion of the mountains provide good farming land. One such plateau, the Franches-Montagnes, lies just east of Switzerland's border with France.

While the Alps are cut through by the many river systems that have long given travelers an easy way through the mountains, the Jura have few natural interruptions. This makes getting across them difficult, and the area has historically been a barrier to settlement.

THE MITTELLAND

Deposits accumulated from the erosion of the Alps over millions of years gradually formed the Mittelland (German for "middle land") region of Switzerland. Also called the Swiss Plateau, this region in the center of the country was also carved by glaciers, but much more gently, to form rolling hills and valleys. Lake Geneva and Lake Constance were formed here as the glaciers hollowed out the lake beds and then melted, leaving the glacial deposits called moraines to block the paths of the meltwater. The Mittelland's average altitude is about 1,500 feet (457 m) above sea level.

The Swiss Plateau makes up about 30 percent of Switzerland's landmass. The great majority of the country's population lives in this region—most Swiss cities are here—which forms Switzerland's main economic area.

RIVERS AND LAKES

Switzerland is considered the hydrographic center of Europe. Both the Rhine and Rhône, two of Europe's biggest rivers, have their sources here. The meltwater from the Alps and the Jura provides the starting point for these great rivers that so many countries in Europe depend on.

The Rhine rises in the Alps and flows first into Lake Constance. As it moves toward the lake, it carries meltwater and mountain streams with it. When it arrives at Lake Constance it is heavily burdened with debris, mud, and gravel. This material remains in the lake. The Rhine emerges again from Lake Constance a green and steady-moving river. The Rhine forms a natural boundary between Switzerland and Germany as far west as Basel, where it leaves Switzerland and begins its journey across Germany.

The Rhône rises in the Rhône glacier in the Furka Pass in the Alps, a few miles away from the source of the Rhine. It descends westward toward Lake Geneva, where it deposits all the material it has carried from the mountainside. At Lake Geneva, it leaves Switzerland behind and becomes a French river, traveling the rest of its journey south along the Jura mountains until it meets the Saône River. Two other important rivers that have their sources in Switzerland are the Ticino, which flows south from the Alps,

and the Reuss, which flows northward. The enormous potential power of Switzerland's glaciers and river systems has been effectively harnessed in power stations that use underground tunnels to carry water and generate electricity. Two of the highest dams in Europe are in Switzerland. They are the Mauvoisin Dam at 777 feet (237 m) and the Grande Dixence Dam at 935 feet (285 m). Both are on the higher reaches of the Rhône and are efficient sources of electrical power.

The Swiss lakes are a major tourist attraction. Lake Geneva, also known as Lac Léman, is a crescent-shaped lake in the west of Switzerland that forms part of the border between Switzerland and France. It is the largest of Switzerland's lakes and is 9 miles (14 km) at its widest point. Several of Switzerland's larger cities are located around the lake, including, of course, Geneva itself. A fleet of ships is maintained on the lake.

Lake Constance forms the eastern boundary of the Mittelland and Switzerland and part of the border with Germany and Austria. It is the second largest lake in Switzerland and is about 40 miles (64 km) long and

Lake Geneva is on the border of Switzerland and France.

The Limmat River flows through Zürich.

8 miles (13 km) wide. The lake's position along the borders gives it a long history as a center for smuggling, but today it is more important as a tourist center. Unlike many other Swiss lakes, it is not surrounded by mountains. The German town of Konstanz (Constance) sits right next to the Swiss town of Kreuzlingen, and border points between the two countries lie a short stroll from the center of both towns. In fact, Konstanz is the only German town on the southern side of Lake Constance.

MAJOR CITIES

ZÜRICH Although it is not the capital of Switzerland, Zürich (or Zuerich) is its largest city and the one that many people believe is the heart of Switzerland. The city is affectionately known to locals as Züri. The city is the economic, industrial, and cultural center of the country and has a population of 390,000, with more than 1.9 million in the greater metropolitan area. Zürich's Kloten Airport is a major international airline travel hub. The city's chief industries are banking and finance, commerce, engineering, electrical appliances, textiles, and tourism. Built around Lake Zürich and the Limmat River, Zürich has been a member of the Swiss Confederation since 1351.

BERN This is the federal capital of Switzerland, with a population of around 139,000. It too is a major industrial center, home to the pharmaceutical industry, the chocolate-making industry, and the printing trades. It has been a member of the Swiss Confederation since 1353. The older part of the city is perched high on a ridge, in a loop of the Aare River. Much of this medieval city is preserved and is a heritage center. Characteristic of the city's shopping centers are arcades that stretch out over the sidewalk, offering pedestrians protection against harsh weather.

The famous clocktower of Bern overlooks a shopping district.

GENEVA This city is built around Lake Geneva and the Rhône. Its major industries include banking, precision instruments, and chemicals. Geneva is the home of more than two hundred international organizations, such as the Red Cross and some of the administrative sections of the United Nations. In fact, Geneva hosts more international organizations than any other city in the world. These organizations' employees, along with other foreign residents, make up a sizeable expatriate community in the city. Out of the 196,000 residents, 48 percent are foreign nationals. Geneva has a long tradition of welcoming foreigners. In the sixteenth and seventeenth centuries many French Protestants fled to Geneva to escape persecution in their home country.

BASEL Situated on the borders of France, Germany, and Switzerland, and located on the banks of the Rhine, Basel is an important center of commerce, communications, and chemical manufacturing. Pharmaceuticals, electrical engineering, and the manufacture of machinery and silk textiles are also important. It is the second largest city in Switzerland and has approximately 174,000 residents. Many of Switzerland's imported goods enter the country via Basel, being transported up the Rhine from Germany and beyond. Basel is a very prosperous city and is home to many of Switzerland's millionaires. The Rhine and its six bridges dominate the city, giving it an almost nautical air, as great barges ply up and down the river.

CLIMATE

Switzerland's climate varies from area to area because of the enormous differences in altitude and the effects of the mountains. As the land rises, temperatures fall by 3 degrees Fahrenheit (2 degrees Celsius) for each 1,000 feet (305 m). In the Mittelland and Alpine valleys, the weather is damper and cloudier than above the cloud line in the high Alps, where the air is dry and there is frequent sunshine. The Swiss Alps have long been a choice location for sanatoriums, where people with various illnesses can recuperate.

In summer, the Mittelland is warm and sunny, with temperatures of 65 to 70°F (18 to 21°C). The sheltered valleys of the Jura and the Alps become hot during the summer months, while the upper slopes are cool. In the region of the Alps that extends toward Italy, the climate is more Mediterranean, with hot summers and mild winters. Switzerland has high precipitation. The Mittelland gets around 45 inches (114 centimeters) of rain per year, while in the higher areas 100 inches (254 cm) of rain per year is common. All precipitation is in areas above 11,500 feet (3,507 m) is snow.

FLORA AND FAUNA

One of Switzerland's greatest natural assets is its many thousands of forests. Fortunately for Switzerland, while other European countries cut down their native oaks and other trees for industry and firewood, the Swiss saw the value of planting.

Switzerland has both deciduous and pine forests. The deciduous forests grow largely in the Jura region, while the mountains of the Alps are covered in natural or planted forests of spruce, larch, and arolla pine trees. The larch is an interesting tree, for unlike the other conifers, it sheds its leaves in the fall instead of winter. Arolla pine trees can live for four hundred years.

Many of the rarer plants of the Swiss Alps are protected by law. The edelweiss is a famous plant that grows high above the tree line in the mountains. It is normally 2 to 12 inches (5 to 30 cm) tall and has white woolly leaves and small yellow flower heads. Other rare Alpine plants are the gentianella, the Alpine pansy, the aster, and the blue thistle.

Switzerland's wildlife is varied and beautiful. But with the encroachment of urban areas, greater use by tourists, and the Swiss love of hunting, many species have become endangered. In 1914 the Swiss National Park was formed in the Engadine area of Graubünden, and some degree of protection was given to the wild creatures of the area. Species of deer that were rare in the early twentieth century have increased to the point where their presence now endangers the survival of some plant species. Ibex were wiped out entirely in the nineteenth century but were reintroduced and are once again wandering the slopes outside the Swiss National Park.

An Alpine chamois is one of several species that are native to the mountains of Europe.

The chamois, a small goat-like antelope, also lives freely in the Alps. It usually stands at a height of 30 inches (76 cm) and weighs 55 to 110 pounds (25 to 50 kilograms). The chamois has vertical horns, black and white markings on the face, and a black tail. It was hunted in earlier times for its soft skin, which was used to make clothing.

INTERNET LINKS

www.swissworld.org/en/geography
The Swiss Federal Department of Foreign Affairs offers an interactive section on Swiss Geography.

www.myswitzerland.com/en-us/home.html
This tourism site has a good section on the country's geography.

HISTORY

The Chateau d'Aigle, or Aigle Castle, in the canton of Vaud, is now a museum.

2

LONG BEFORE SWITZERLAND WAS Switzerland, people lived in this Alpine region. Evidence of human habitation dates back thirty thousand years or more to the Paleolithic age. Humans subsisted by hunting animals and gathering wild plants. Cutting tools that probably belonged to Neanderthals have been found in a cave in Neuchâtel. Later, people of the Neolithic age settled in the Rhône and Rhine valleys. They practiced agriculture and raised livestock. Around 1,800 BCE, Bronze Age people settled in the Mittelland and Alpine valleys and shaped bronze and copper into tools and weapons.

By the late Iron Age, a great new center of culture had emerged on the banks of Lake Neuchâtel: the La Tène civilization of the Celts, a warlike race that swept across Europe. In what is now Switzerland, the Celts lived in the area between Lake Constance and Lake Geneva, on the Jura, and in the Alps.

For centuries, Switzerland has been a neutral country, which means that it cannot take part in armed conflict unless it is attacked. Nevertheless, it maintains a military for purposes of self-defense and internal security. The tradition of a citizen army is seen as an essential requirement of Swiss neutrality.

UNDER FOREIGN RULE

By the time recorded history began, the Celts in Switzerland, called Helvetians, were facing border threats by powerful tribes from Germany. The Helvetians tried to emigrate to Gaul in an area that is now France. However they found their way barred by the Romans under Julius Caesar, then governor of Gaul.

The Romans wanted the Helvetians to stay where they were to provide a barrier between the Roman Empire and the waves of invading Germanic peoples from the north. In 58 BCE the Romans stopped the Helvetians at ancient Bibracte in Burgundy (France) and defeated them. The Helvetians were forced to retreat to what was to be called *Helvetia* (hehl-VAYT-see-ah), the area between Lake Constance and Lake Geneva. They were promised protection from the Germanic peoples by the Romans, and Helvetia became a province in the massive Roman Empire. Under the Romans, Helvetia developed rapidly. Road networks were built, towns were reestablished, and agriculture flourished.

Julius Caesar, left, encounters Divico, a Gallic king and leader of the Helvetians, after the Battle of the Saône in 58 BCE.

THE EARLY CHRISTIANS

One of the first groups of Christians to arrive in Switzerland was a band of Irish monks, led by Columban (right), in 610 CE. An early chronicle described the monks as long-haired and tattooed, carrying stout sticks, and a spare pair of boots around their necks. They traveled around Switzerland throwing carved images of gods into the rivers and causing havoc among the population, who resented their high-handed attempts to Christianize them. Driven out of the lakeside village of Tuggan, the monks moved into Brigantium (modern Bregenz) and began to smash heathen gods. Again ordered out of the area, the monks moved into Italy, leaving behind one of their number, Gall, who was too sick to make the journey. In 612 CE Gall founded a monastery on the site of the present-day Saint Gallen.

A region to the east of Helvetia was inhabited by people who were related to the Etruscans and Celtics. Following Roman conquest of this area, spoken Latin mixed with the area's existing languages, resulting in a Rhaetian version of vulgar Latin. Through the centuries, this language has developed to become what we know as today's Romansh.

Germanic peoples began invading Switzerland in 259 CE, and Roman rule in the country finally crumbled in 400 CE. The Celts were displaced by Germanic peoples, mainly Burgundians and Alemannians. The Burgundians settled in the western part of Switzerland. The vulgar Latin spoken in this area gradually evolved into a French dialect. This area is in the French-speaking section of present-day Switzerland. The Alemannians settled in the northern part of the country, which is the German-speaking section of Switzerland. The Rhaetians resisted the Alemannians and remained in Graubünden canton until today. The southern parts of Switzerland came under the influence of Italy. Therefore, four different power groups developed, each with its own language.

In the sixth century, Switzerland became part of the Frankish kingdom ruled by Clovis, the first Germanic king to convert to Christianity. By 800 CE,

Switzerland was part of the Holy Roman Empire under Charles the Great, later called Charlemagne. It was under his rule that the modern cantons of Switzerland were largely created. By 843 CE, Switzerland was split among Charlemagne's grandsons. It was not until 1032 that the Swiss territories were once more brought under a single ruler, the Holy Roman Emperor Conrad II. During the twelfth century, Switzerland was again divided up and fought over. By 1291, Switzerland had come under the power of the House of Habsburg, which was to rule the Holy Roman Empire for nearly four hundred years.

THE FOUNDATION OF MODERN SWITZERLAND

As an outcome of the increased power of the Habsburgs, a desire for autonomy and freedom was born in some of the cantons that would later become Switzerland. For the first time they saw a common goal of independence from emperors.

In 1291 Emperor Rudolf of Habsburg died, and in the vacuum created by his death, some of the Swiss cantons decided to act. Three of them, Uri, Schwyz, and Unterwalden, drew up a defense agreement called the Perpetual Covenant, pledging mutual aid and allegiance. They instituted guerrilla attacks on the bailiffs and soldiers of the Habsburg Empire. One of the Habsburg dukes led a force against the united cantons in 1315 but was defeated by them. This led to a whole spate of other cantons joining the Confederation—Lucerne in 1332, Zürich in 1351, Glarus and Zug in 1352, and Bern in 1353. The Swiss fought and defeated the Habsburgs in 1386 and 1388.

THE CONFEDERATION EXPANDS

The Confederation of eight Swiss states began to look to expansion as their best defense. In the early fifteenth century, they took more land from the Habsburg Empire, while other Swiss cantons decided to declare their own independence without joining the Confederation. This group negotiated a temporary peace with the Habsburgs and instead took land from the Burgundian Empire. War against Burgundy began in 1474. In March 1476,

WILLIAM TELL

No one can quite decide whether the story of William Tell is Swiss history or Swiss myth. Perhaps it's best described as a legend, in that it might have its roots in history but over time has taken on mythic qualities. Whichever it is, it's a good tale and is as much a part of the character of Switzerland as cheese or cuckoo clocks.

William Tell's story begins during Emperor Rudolf's reign. Tell's canton was governed by the ruthless Habsburg supervisor Gessler, who, the story goes, put his hat on a pole in the town center and made everybody who passed that spot bow to it. He also confiscated land from the Swiss, robbing them of huge sources of income in rents and tithes, and insulted them. When Tell refused to bow to the hat, a series of insults passed between the two men. Gessler forced Tell to shoot an apple off his son's head. Tell, who was known for his excellent aim, knocked the apple off with no injury to his child. He told Gessler, however, that had the boy died, Tell's second arrow would have been for him. Infuriated, Gessler had Tell arrested. En route to jail, Tell escaped and killed Gessler.

That sparked a rebellion which led to the birth of Swiss Confederation. Tell became a national hero and a symbol of freedom. The story inspired many works of art, among them the opera William Tell *by Gioachino Rossini, best known for its famous overture.*

A sculpture of Huldrich Zwingli preaching to the masses adorns the bronze doors of the Grossmünster, a Romanesque Protestant church in Zürich.

a Burgundian army was defeated by a Swiss force at Grandson, and later that year in Morat, both towns in western Switzerland. Throughout the war, the reputation of the Swiss as soldiers grew. But as the Confederation took more and more land, they began to quarrel among themselves. In 1481, on the verge of civil war, they signed a new pact and drew two new cantons into the Confederation. Now a Confederation of ten states, they were joined in the next thirty years by three more.

The Confederation began to grow rich, partly on the spoils of the many battles its mercenaries began to undertake on behalf of foreign kingdoms. Although Switzerland today stands for neutrality, for many years there were no major wars in Europe that did not have Swiss soldiers fighting on one side or another. The chief export of Switzerland became soldiers, and as their military prowess grew, so did the wealth of the city cantons. But this was not to last. Other countries learned the lessons of the Swiss mercenaries and set up competing mercenary forces. Warfare underwent a massive change during this century, and the high cost of military equipment began to make the prospect of peace more financially rewarding to European rulers.

THE REFORMATION

At the start of the sixteenth century things were in decline for the Swiss Confederation, which now consisted of thirteen states and several occupied territories. Their reputation as mercenaries had declined, there was less demand for troops all over Europe, and they had been badly defeated by the French in the battle of Marignano in 1515.

Worse was to come in the form of the Reformation. It established the division between politics and religion in Europe and wrought dramatic changes all over the continent. None, however, were as affected as Switzerland.

The Reformation, led by Martin Luther in Germany, was a crusade against what was seen as corrupt practices in the Roman Catholic Church. Chief among these were the way in which the Church involved itself in secular matters, its financial corruption, and the ceremonies and furnishings of the Church itself that had become ostentatious, with the acquisition of paintings, statues, and valuable artifacts.

In Switzerland, the reforms were led by Huldrych Zwingli (HOOLD-ryke TSVING-lee), who saw the religious changes as part of a larger picture, the reform of society, starting in Zürich. He believed that in order to build a new society, it was necessary to destroy the old one. Zürich had long had a very bad reputation, and the city council was pleased to encourage him in his reforms. All decorations were thrown out of the churches, and in 1523 the Catholic rites were abolished in favor of Protestant services. The rural cantons surrounding Zürich did not go along with these changes and issued warrants for Zwingli's arrest. This led to war between the city's forces and the rural cantons in 1531. In the ensuing battle Zwingli was killed.

This engraved portrait of John Calvin dates to 1858.

In Geneva, a French reformer named John Calvin was influential. His religious beliefs were more extreme than Zwingli's but concentrated on the church alone rather than interfering in state affairs.

The shock waves of the Reformation continued to affect Europe for another century. Before the end of the Reformation, there was one last destructive convulsion. This was the Thirty Years' War, a series of wars fought first over religion and later for territory and power. Although the Swiss Confederation remained neutral, the basic divisions that had opened up between the Protestant urban cantons and the rural Catholic ones meant that the cantons supported different parties in the wars.

When the Thirty Years' War ended in 1648, the rest of Europe acknowledged Switzerland as an independent confederation of states. The seventeenth and eighteenth centuries were marked by industrialization, which brought economic prosperity to Switzerland. The neutrality that the Swiss maintained during the Thirty Years' War helped to safeguard their economy. Refugees who fled to Switzerland also contributed to the economic growth, because they brought with them useful skills in watchmaking and textiles.

NAPOLEON INVADES

In 1798, during the French Revolution, French military forces invaded Switzerland under the leadership of their emperor, Napoleon Bonaparte. Switzerland became a French satellite state and was named the Helvetic Republic. Internal discord, however, brought about the demise of the Republic, which lasted only five years.

In 1803, Bonaparte enforced a settlement on the Republic, giving it some sovereignty and enlisting six of the previous vassal states as members. These nineteen cantons formed the Helvetic Confederation. In 1815, after more wrangling between the cantons, three more of the vassal states became full members of the Confederation. By now there were twenty-two cantons in the Confederation. It was during this period, too, that Switzerland's neutrality was recognized internationally.

A NEW CONSTITUTION

Starting in 1830, liberal constitutions were drawn up in twelve cantons. The year 1847 saw the end of a brief civil war between the Catholic cantons and the other Swiss cantons. The Catholic cantons broke off to form a separate government called the Sonderbund. In 1848 this dispute resulted in the drawing up of a new constitution. The rest of Europe continued in a state of turmoil for much of the nineteenth century, but the Swiss Confederation had finally found a means of peacefully coexisting, while remaining neutral in European and world affairs. The last canton to join the Confederation was the Jura in 1974.

SWISS NEUTRALITY AND THE TWO WORLD WARS

With many clearly differentiated cultural groups, Switzerland's neutrality and even its existence as an independent state was continually at risk. During the Franco-Prussian War of 1870—1871, German Swiss supported Prussia, while French Swiss supported France. In 1914 the assassination of Archduke Ferdinand, which set in motion a chain of events that resulted in World War I,

A DARKER VIEW OF SWISS NEUTRALITY

Switzerland's neutrality would have meant nothing if Germany or some other aggressor had decided to invade. In fact, there is evidence that Adolf Hitler had such a plan, but never acted on it. That fact raises the question: Did Switzerland make itself sufficiently useful to Germany in some other way? The shining image of neutral Switzerland as the safe haven in the sea of World War II's horror and chaos has been tarnished by the answer to that question.

Recent revelations about Switzerland's wartime transactions with Germany more than suggest its culpability. The country served as a convenient place to hide Jewish assets stolen by the Nazis. Gold, diamonds, cash, artworks, and other valuables were stashed in Swiss bank accounts and safe deposit boxes. (The plunder even included gold dental fillings extracted from corpses.) At the end of the war, Switzerland resisted Allied demands to return the funds to their rightful owners. The country finally agreed to return a mere 12 percent of the stolen gold. For the most part, Holocaust survivors or their families were unable to reclaim their property from Swiss banking officials, who imposed impenetrable bureaucratic barriers.

Kaspar Villiger

Meanwhile, many European Jews had also transferred their assets to Swiss banks, thinking it would be safe there until after the war. The Swiss were happy to accept Jewish money, but not as willing to accept the Jews themselves. Jewish refugees fleeing the Holocaust were routinely and vigorously denied admission to Switzerland. Many would go on to die instead in the German concentration camps.

Today, Switzerland is being forced to face its dark history. Evidence shows that the Swiss profited greatly from both the victims of the Holocaust and their executioners—a "neutrality" that was far from benign. In 1995, when Swiss Federal President Kaspar Villiger said, "we bear a considerable burden of guilt for the treatment of Jews by our country," it was the first admission by a Swiss government leader of any wrongdoing during those war years.

An employee handles Swiss francs and euro notes on the counter of a currency exchange in Switzerland.

brought all the French-German tensions back to the forefront of Swiss life. Shortly after the war began, Swiss neutrality was threatened when it was discovered that German sympathizers were passing military secrets to the German side. The Swiss soldiers who patrolled the borders were not compensated for lost wages, leading to unrest in the ranks. The Swiss economy also felt the pinch of the war. Large numbers of refugees fled into Switzerland.

After the war, with its neutrality intact, Switzerland faced the dilemma of whether it could remain neutral and still join the newly formed League of Nations, the predecessor of the United Nations. Switzerland finally joined the League in 1920 as one of its original members. The seat, or headquarters, of the organization was moved to Geneva later that year and remained there until the League disbanded in 1946.

When World War II began to take shape, Switzerland was given special dispensation to ignore any trade sanctions against Germany. For the duration of the war, Switzerland traded with both the Allies and the Axis powers. Its borders were patrolled by 650,000 troops, and the Alps became the designated spot where German invading troops would be met and stopped. Switzerland planned to have its key facilities blown up should a German invasion occur. The Saint Gotthard Tunnel, a major artery through the Alps, was one of the facilities earmarked for destruction. Although it was later discovered that Germany had made plans for an invasion of Switzerland, it never took place, and Switzerland emerged from World War II with a booming economy among the ruins of the rest of Europe. It was thus perfectly placed to benefit from the enormous needs of reconstructing Europe. After World War II, Switzerland reverted to complete neutrality by refusing to join the United Nations, since doing so would mean possible involvement in military commitments. Nonetheless, some important UN agencies are based in Geneva, and in 2002 Switzerland finally became a full member.

In more recent times, Switzerland has experienced other challenges to its stability. It became one of the last European states to grant women the vote and experienced a huge influx of foreign workers and refugees. So far, Switzerland has chosen not to join the European Union. It does, however, have a relationship with the EU, framed by various treaties that allow it to participate in the EU's single market. As a result, the EU is Switzerland's largest trading partner. But recent political developments in Switzerland may threaten that relationship. For example, in 2014, the Swiss voted in a referendum to impose quotas on all immigrants. It was an attempt to slow large-scale immigration, but doing so breaks some EU treaty stipulations.

INTERNET LINKS

www.swissinfo.ch/eng/lake-dwellings-reveal-hidden-past/30542748
"Lake dwellings reveal hidden past" discusses the remains of prehistoric villages found underwater in lake areas of Switzerland.

www.bbc.com/news/world-europe-17988450
BBC News offers a timeline of key events in Swiss history from 1291 to the present.

www.nytimes.com/1997/01/26/weekinreview/the-not-so-neutrals-of-world-war-ii.html
"The (Not So) Neutrals of World War II" argues that neutrality (Swiss and others) in WWII was not a clear-cut construct.

www.lonelyplanet.com/switzerland/history
This is a good, basic overview of Swiss history.

www.smithsonianmag.com/history/in-search-of-william-tell-2198511
The *Smithsonian* article "In Search of William Tell" tries to determine the historical truth behind the legend.

In Switzerland, as in thirteen other European countries today, it is illegal to deny that the Holocaust happened. It is a crime punishable by imprisonment to "deny, grossly minimize, or seek to justify genocide or other crimes against humanity."

GOVERNMENT

The Federal Palace in Bern, the capital of Switzerland, can be seen from the River Aare.

3

THE SWISS GOVERNMENT IS UNLIKE any other. It is the closest thing the world has to a direct democracy—it is perhaps more accurate to call it a semi-direct democracy. Its head of state and head of government is a group of seven people. Citizens in this sort of democracy have more power than in the more typical representative democracy. Whether the Swiss system would work in a larger nation is debated by political scientists, but it has been working for Switzerland since 1848.

THE CONSTITUTION

Before 1848 the Swiss Confederation consisted of a loose organization of twenty-five independent cantons, each with its own system of government, ranging from democracy to oligarchy and aristocracy.

The 1848 Constitution set up a Republican government. It gave control of foreign affairs to the federal government, imposed democratic government on all the cantons, and banned the hiring out of mercenary armies. The Constitution was revised in 1874 and has been adjusted many times by referendum. The Constitution was fully revised in 1999 and implemented in January 2000.

In Switzerland, there are three levels of government: the federal level, the cantons, and the communes.

The official portrait of the Swiss Federal Council for 2015 shows Simonetta Sommaruga (*foreground, right*), president of the Confederation for 2015, and Johann Schneider-Ammann (*foreground, left*), vice president.

THE FEDERAL GOVERNMENT

At the federal level, the Swiss government operates on the principal of the separation of powers. This prevents the concentration of power in any one individual or group. Power is shared between three independent entities: the legislature (Parliament), which makes laws; the executive (Federal Council), which implements the laws; and the judiciary (Supreme Court), which administers justice. No one can belong to more than one of the three federal authorities at the same time.

THE EXECUTIVE The highest authority is the Federal Council. Each of its seven members is responsible for a government department—defense, transportation and energy, justice and the police, the economy, finance, foreign affairs, and the interior. The Federal Council also represents the Swiss Confederation at home and abroad. Three of the political parties are represented by two seats each, while the fourth has one seat. No two members can come from the same canton. In 1984 the first woman was elected to the council. The Federal Council is elected every four years. It is known abroad as the cabinet.

Every year, a new president of the Federation is chosen from among the members of the Federal Council. The president's job is largely ceremonial. He or she is supported by the Presidential Affairs Unit, which was established in 2015. This unit mainly provides foreign policy advice.

THE LEGISLATURE The Parliament is a bicameral, or two chamber, body. The two houses are the National Council, similar in function to the U.S. House of Representatives, and the Council of States, similar in function to the Senate. The National Council has two hundred members elected for a four-

DEMOCRACY—DIRECT OR REPRESENTATIVE?

Most of the world's democracies, including the United States, have a representative form of government. That is, the people vote for officials to act for them in the running of the country. In the United States, citizens vote for senators and congress members to formulate government policy. In this form of government, majority opinion may dominate, but minority factions are usually ensured some form of representation.

In a direct, or pure, democracy, on the other hand, the people themselves determine policy. Typically, they do this through a direct form of voting called a referendum, or through some other way of coming to consensus. This form of democracy gives citizens more power, and is based on the rule of the majority; it has few or no provisions for minority voices.

In Switzerland, it's a bit more complicated. Citizens do elect representatives, but also have the means to vote directly. Referenda are held on the most important issues. All men and—since 1971, women—age eighteen and above have the right to vote.

At the federal level, the right of initiative enables any citizen to propose a change to the Constitution. If 100,000 electors sign a proposed constitutional change, the federal government can make a counterproposal and a popular vote is taken on the issue.

The citizens also have a right to demand a referendum on any new piece of legislation. If 50,000 electors or eight cantons demand a referendum within one hundred days of a new piece of legislation being published, the referendum will be held. If the voters decide against it, the legislation is dropped or altered.

year term by proportional representation. The Council of States has forty-six members selected by the cantons.

Although elections to all these bodies take place every four years, the Swiss voter probably has more selections to make than in any other democracy. Referenda are common occurrences, with voting and elections held on weekends to cause as little disruption as possible.

THE JUDICIARY The Federal Court is the supreme arbiter of justice in Switzerland and is based in Lausanne. Its function is mainly as a court of appeal on judgments passed by the cantonal courts. Its judgments on cases become the law of the land. Other judges at lower levels must use the Supreme Court's judgments as models for their own. The Federal Court also arbitrates disputes between the cantons.

LOCAL GOVERNMENT

CANTONS Switzerland is divided into twenty-six cantons. All but one were originally the states that united in 1848 to form the Confederation. The other, the Jura, was created in 1979 when it separated from the canton of Bern.

Under the Federal Constitution, all cantons have equal rights, and a high degree of independence. Each canton has its own constitution, as well as its own government, parliament, and courts. Each canton elects a government of around seven members, in most cases by a direct majority system. Direct democracy in the form of a People's Assembly still exists only in the cantons of Appenzell Innerrhoden and Glarus. In all others, the citizens vote by mail or at the ballot box.

The people elect members of their canton parliaments by way of a system of proportional representation. The size of each parliament varies between 50 and 180 members. Parliamentary elections are held on average every four years, again depending on the canton. The parliaments are empowered to collect taxes and decide on matters of health, education, and social services.

COMMUNES At the administrative level below the canton, Switzerland is divided into 2,324 communes. These are the smallest of the country's political entities. Communes are the smallest political units in Switzerland. The number of communes is declining as some smaller communes merge together to share resources more efficiently.

About 20 percent of the communes have their own parliament, especially those made up of towns or cities. The rest still make direct democratic decisions at communal assemblies.

Communal governments are responsible for tax collection and matters relating to schools, social services, fire departments, energy supplies, road construction, and local planning.

A Landsgemeinde takes place in Appenzell Innerrhoden.

THE LANDSGEMEINDE

The *Landsgemeinde* (LAHNTS-geh-min-de), an outdoor assembly of people gathered for the purpose of conducting government business, is an ancient tradition dating back to the fourteenth century. Once, all the cantons elected their leaders in this way, but now it is practiced in only two cantons. Every spring, on the last Sunday in April or the first Sunday in May, the voters of Glarus and Appenzell Innerrhoden hold an open-air meeting in the main squares of their capital towns to vote on a host of local issues. The residents may vote on the legislation, judges and cantonal representatives, permits, infrastructure, and so on. Voting is by a show of hands.

In Appenzell Innerrhoden, the Landsgemeinde is a festive day. The town square, where the voting takes place, is decorated with colorful flags. There are also stalls selling special Landsgemeinde pastries. The event starts with a church service.

FOREIGN POLICY

Switzerland long ago decided that, surrounded as it was by potential aggressors, its safest form of defense was neutrality. Switzerland's neutrality was accepted at the 1815 Congress of Vienna and in the 1919 Treaty of

POLITICAL PARTIES

A two-party political system, such as is found in the United States, does not exist in Switzerland. As a matter of custom, each party is represented on the Federal Council so no one political group can really dominate or determine policy. There are different parties represented in the National Council, ranging from the four main parties—the Christian Democrats (centrist), the Radical Party (center-right), the Social Democrats (left-wing), and the Swiss People's Party (conservative right)—to environmentalist groups and independents. The fact that the parties are able to cooperate so easily in government shows that they have very few major differences. In recent years, the conservative Swiss People's Party has become the strongest political party in Switzerland.

In addition to this type of political grouping, the system allows for pressure groups to form. Because of the citizens' rights to call for a referendum on national issues, groups form continuously in order to force discussion on certain topics. Conservationists, the anti-nuclear lobby, anti-fascist groups, and anti-abortion groups have all used their rights to call for a referendum on the issues they think are important.

Simonetta Sommaruga of the Social Democrats is elected in 2010.

Versailles. But neutrality is not an easy position to hold in a world where increasingly countries are forming alliances in order to survive. Switzerland cannot enter any international agreement that might oblige the country to come to another's aid. It is not a part of NATO and became part of the United Nations only in 2002. Even now, Switzerland is not yet a part of the European Union. This is partly due to the country's desire to protect its domestic industries but even more so due to its political need to remain neutral.

Although Switzerland does not take sides in international disputes, the country puts a great deal of effort into its foreign policy. Switzerland spends huge sums on international aid to developing countries and has a relief corps that is dispatched to any natural disaster. Switzerland also provides an international service via the International Red Cross, maintaining a fleet of aircraft to be dispatched anywhere in the world where there are war casualties. During World War II, Switzerland opened its borders to 300,000 refugees. Geneva is also home to many international organizations that are involved in human rights and humanitarian international law, such as the World Health Organization (WHO). In addition, Switzerland maintains political relations with as many countries as possible and often acts as a go-between or mediator between countries that have cut off political relations with one another but still need to communicate.

Over the years, however, many people have criticized Switzerland's stance on neutrality, which has often proved to be lucrative. While their neighbors were at war, Switzerland has traded with both sides.

The entrance to the United Nations building in Geneva is lined with flags from around the world.

INTERNET LINKS

www.admin.ch
The official site of the Swiss federal government in English explains the government structure and has a link to an excellent PDF brochure.

www.vtg.admin.ch/internet/vtg/en/home.html
The government site of the Swiss Armed Forces has information in English.

www.swissinfo.ch/eng/political-parties/29288918
The Swissinfo site explains the positions of the country's major political parties.

ECONOMY

Old clockwork demonstrates that Switzerland has long been known for its elite clock and watchmaking industries.

4

SWITZERLAND IS SMALL. IT HAS no access to the sea. Much of its land is mountainous and therefore unsuitable for agriculture. Its people can't even converse with one another in one language. One could easily expect such a place to be struggling economically. And yet, Switzerland has done very well over the years. It's fair to say it is a wealthy country; it has one of the highest standards of living in the world.

Beginning in the Middle Ages, Switzerland's chief export was a group of well-trained soldiers who would fight for whichever king paid them the most. Switzerland grew rich on the spoils of war. After the battles of Grandson and Morat in 1476, when the Swiss routed the Burgundian armies, huge hauls of booty were taken that included enormous diamonds, silks, and plain hard cash. Swiss neutrality in later years ensured that these resources were never lost.

During the Thirty Years' War in the seventeenth century, the Swiss grew rich by trading with the belligerents, supplying cereals, vegetables, and meat to countries so war-torn that they could not grow their own food. Switzerland also took in refugees whose skills began the Swiss tradition of producing tiny intricate objects such as watches and jewels.

Today Switzerland has thriving banking, watchmaking, chocolate, tourism, chemical, engineering, and pharmaceutical industries. Building

The Swatch Group, formed in 1983, is a Swiss watch manufacturer based in Biel. It owns numerous Swiss watch and jewelry brands. It also introduced the popular, artsy, and inexpensive Swatch watch in the 1980s.

In 2015, one of the world's largest private Swatch collections sold at auction for $6 million. The collection, with more than 5,800 Swatches collected over twenty-five years, was sold to an unnamed European institution.

on its centuries-long pedagogical tradition, Switzerland is also famous for a great number of international educational institutions. Students from all over the world attend these schools.

AGRICULTURE

Two-thirds of Switzerland's landmass is rock, water, or forest. Urban growth uses up another large chunk of the potential agricultural land so that only about 10 percent of the total land surface is used for agriculture.

The number of people involved in agricultural production has declined rapidly. In the nineteenth century, 60 percent of the population worked in agriculture. By World War II, this had dropped to 22 percent, and it is now about 3.4 percent. This does not mean, however, that agricultural production has dropped. Farms are now much larger than they once were and are highly mechanized. Agriculture contributes 0.7 percent of the GDP.

In the mountain regions, the chief activity is raising livestock, mostly cattle. In the central plateau and lower Alpine valleys, grapevines, vegetables,

A farmer and cheesemaker poses with his cows in La Lecherette in the Swiss Alps.

and tobacco are grown in addition to livestock. Dairy production dominates Swiss agriculture. Milk production is at a surplus, and cheese and chocolate, both milk products, are exported. Swiss vineyards produce an average of 29 million gallons (1.1 hectoliters) of wine every year. Grapes are grown in Ticino, the valleys of the Rhône, and near Lake Geneva, Lake Neuchâtel, Lake Biel, and Lake Zürich.

Many agricultural products are protected by the government against cheaper imports by means of import tariffs, and fixed prices paid to farmers for certain agricultural products. This need to protect the domestic agricultural industry is one of the chief reasons Switzerland has been reluctant to be a part of the European Union.

A tram passes through the mountain of the Matterhorn, a top tourist attraction in Switzerland.

MACHINERY AND ELECTRONICS

The machine, electronics, and metallurgical industries account for a major part of Switzerland's total exports. About 26 percent of the total workforce is employed in these industries. The Swiss machine industry includes everything from machine tools and precision instruments to heavy electrical equipment. The machine tool industry originally developed out of the needs of Switzerland's own textile industry, which peaked during the nineteenth century. The development of railways, hydroelectric power, and the motorization of seagoing vessels all called for complex machinery, which was developed in Switzerland. The Swiss built the first electric track railway, the first turbogenerator, the first pump turbine, and the first gas turbine power station. As electronics have become more important in industry, Swiss technology has kept pace.

WATCHMAKING

French refugees of the sixteenth century first brought skills to Switzerland that made possible the development of the watch industry. The first watchmakers' guild in Switzerland was established in the seventeenth century in Geneva. From there the industry spread out along the Jura Mountains to Schaffhausen. Mass production of tiny parts began in Switzerland in 1845, long before other countries had the technology, so Switzerland gained an enormous advantage over other watchmaking areas.

In 1921 the Swiss Laboratory of Horological Research was set up so Swiss manufacturers could pool ideas. In 1967 the first quartz watch was manufactured in Switzerland. Liquid crystal displays (LCDs), electro-chromic displays, combined analog and digital displays, and optic sensors were all developed in Switzerland.

Every year 90 percent of the watch industry's production is exported all over the world, generating an average annual revenue of 21 billion Swiss francs (US $21.7 billion). Overall, Switzerland exported 28.6 million watches in 2014, almost half a million more than in 2013. More than half of those went to Asia, 31 percent to Europe, and 14 percent to the United States. However, with China exporting more than 600 million watches a year, Switzerland is stressing the quality of its brand. The average Swiss-made watch cost around $700 (676 francs), and the average Chinese-made watch costs about $2. With such a price difference, the Swiss are mainly in the luxury market, which they dominate.

CHEMICALS AND PHARMACEUTICALS

The Swiss chemical industry, like the machine tool industry, developed out of the needs of the textile factories of the nineteenth century. Dyes were needed for the woven cloth, and so the dyestuff industry developed. Today, dyes are made for cloth, leather, paper, paints, and varnishes.

The pharmaceutical industry is very capital-intensive. Each new drug takes at least twelve years of research and testing before it can be put on the market. Roche, Novartis, Syngenta, Clariant, Givaudan, Meyhall, and Ciba are all Swiss-based pharmaceutical firms with research and processing plants in many parts of the world.

Textiles by Swiss fabric designer Jakob Schlaepfer are displayed in the company showroom in St. Gallen.

TEXTILES

Fabric and lace are two of the oldest manufactured goods in Switzerland. The textile industry dates back to the Middle Ages when spinning and weaving were the dominant professions in certain towns. Silk was associated with Zürich, drapery with Fribourg, and linen and cotton with Saint Gall. These were cottage industries, with small home workshops producing materials for the towns' buyers. Even now, textile companies are small compared to other industries and are still decentralized.

The textile industry relies on a good export market and is susceptible to economic downturns in other countries. After World War II, for example, the embroidery industry, which had employed 100,000 people in the northeastern cantons, was virtually wiped out. But the industry has regained some of its former strength.

Switzerland is also a leading manufacturer of textile machinery, with an estimated global market share of 33 percent.

THE SWISS ARMY KNIFE: A TOOL FOR ALL REASONS

In 1884, Karl Elsener opened a surgical equipment shop in Ibach-Schywz and was soon commissioned to produce a new pocketknife for the Swiss Army. The army needed a simple folding knife that could be used both to open canned food and to assemble and disassemble the Swiss service rifle. At the time, that process required a screwdriver. The first such knives had been produced by a German manufacturer, and consisted of a single blade, a reamer, a can opener, and a screwdriver. Its handle was black.

When Elsener took over production of the knife in 1891, he improved upon its design. He created a way for the tools to be attached on both sides of the handle using a spring mechanism. This innovation allowed him to use the same spring to hold all the tools in place, and he was able to put twice as many features on the knife. He also made the handle red, so it would stand out in the snow.

Since then, the Swiss Army knife has become popular around the world—and beyond. A knife went into space with the crew of the Space Shuttle, and an oversized copy is on display in New York's Museum of Modern Art. Infinitely practical and beautifully designed, it is an icon of Switzerland itself.

The knives are now produced by two Swiss companies: Victorinox and Wenger. Each knife features the Swiss flag cross logo and the national coat of arms. The knives also come with a wide range of tools, including various screwdrivers, corkscrew and bottle openers, key ring, tweezers, toothpick, scissors, multi-purpose hook, wrench, wood saw, fish scaler, ruler, orange peeler, chisel, magnifying lens, pliers, pressurized ballpoint pen, nail clippers, window breaker, seat belt cutter, laser pointer, USB flash drive, MP3 player, fingerprint scanner with built-in data encryption—and many other of life's little necessities.

TOURISM

Switzerland has been a magnet for tourists since the eighteenth century, when geologist Horace Saussure published an ode to the Alps, praising their beauty. Switzerland has clean air, beautiful scenery, winter and other sports, lots of history, and plenty of culture. It's one of the top twenty-five tourist destinations in the world. More than eight million foreign tourists visit the country every year.

Tourism employs one of the largest workforces in the country. In 2011, tourism accounted for about 2.9 percent of Switzerland GDP, making it the fourth largest source of revenue after the machine, metal, chemical, and watchmaking industries.

Switzerland tourism is not limited to the summer season. Winter offers activities such as skiing, sledding, tobogganing, and ice-skating, while summer brings golf, boating, walking, and climbing. The major winter resorts are Saint-Moritz, Gstaad, Interlaken, Chambéry, Davos, and Zermatt.

Tourism has had a beneficial effect on the country in ways other than national income. Regions that might have become depopulated have developed as tourist areas; chalets and cottages that might have fallen into ruin have become holiday homes.

But there are drawbacks. Demand for new ski resorts and hotels have made claims on an already shrinking countryside. Laws have been introduced to control the design of the new resorts and to protect endangered species. Visitors are now encouraged to visit during the less busy seasons—spring and fall.

BANKING

Perhaps Switzerland's most famous—or infamous—industry is banking. The idea of saving for the future is deeply rooted in Swiss society and has given rise to a unique financial network. Many foreign investors use Swiss banks, attracted by laws regarding secrecy and the stability of Swiss society. Investors can make use of numbered bank accounts, whose ownership is known only to a few people. Today about one-third of all worldwide funds that are held

Switzerland built its reputation with a 1934 law making it a crime for banks to reveal a client's identity. Intentionally or not, Swiss banks became a safe haven for the interests of a wide variety of criminals. Organized crime, tax cheats, money launderers, terrorist organizations, and international tyrants and thugs of all stripes have been suspected of hiding their ill-begotten assets behind the respectable but impermeable façade of the Swiss banks.

Most notoriously, the banks are accused of aiding the Nazis and benefiting from the victims of World War II. Switzerland claimed neutrality during WWII and therefore thousands of people, including many Jews, deposited their money in Switzerland. When the depositors died, most of them at the hands of the Nazis, their relatives were often denied any access to their funds, funds that the banks continued to make interest off. The banks are also said to have funneled hundreds of millions into Nazi Germany, perhaps in return for not being invaded by it.

Today things are changing. In 2013, Swiss President Ueli Maurer defended banking secrecy, saying it is comparable to medical confidentiality. "The state must absolutely respect the private sphere," he said, "[and should not know] what there is in your bank account." Nevertheless, pressure from the United States and the European Union has persuaded the Swiss to align its bank practices with those of other countries.

outside their country of origin (a situation called "offshore" funds) are kept in Switzerland. In 2007, Swiss banks managed about $2.7 trillion dollars.

In 2009, the financial sector comprised 11.6 percent of Switzerland's GDP and employed approximately 195,000 people (136,000 of whom work in the banking sector). This represents about 5.6 percent of the total Swiss workforce. In addition, Swiss banks employ about 103,000 people abroad.

FOREIGN WORKERS

For many years the rate of increase of the Swiss population has not kept up with the needs of industry and so workers from other countries, chiefly neighboring European ones, have come to live in the country. Apart from expatriates, there are also guest workers from Italy, Spain, and Portugal. They provide the low-paid manual labor needed to construct some of Switzerland's major infrastructure projects, such as highways.

Switzerland has benefited a great deal in the past from the influx of foreign workers and refugees from European wars. The official figures for foreign workers are actually lower than the real ones since there are many people living near the Swiss borders who commute into Switzerland for work. Many seasonal workers, too, move to tourist areas such as Lugano just for one season before returning to Italy or Spain.

INTERNET LINKS

www.myswitzerland.com/en-us/textile-crafts.html
The "Textile crafts" section of this site includes interesting historical information.

www.fhs.ch/eng/homepage.html
This is the home site of the Federation of the Swiss Watch Industry.

www.swissarmy.com/us
The home page of Victorinox has a history of the iconic knife and a selection of what's available today.

www.myswitzerland.com/en-us/home.html
The main Swiss tourism site has a wealth of information about the country itself.

www.economist.com/node/21547229
"Don't Ask, Won't Tell" is an article from the *Economist* about Swiss banking secrecy.

ENVIRONMENT

A pristine alpine landscape in eastern Switzerland is as environmentally healthy as it looks.

SWITZERLAND IS ONE OF THE "greenest" countries in the industrialized world. The Swiss have long taken a commendably active stance in support of the environment and against pollution. In 2014, the country topped the annual Environmental Performance Index (EPI), an environmental scorecard which ranks countries on high-priority environmental concerns including air quality, water management, and climate change. Switzerland got top marks for its performance in the categories of water and sanitation, water resources, biodiversity and habitat, and health impacts. It needs improvement, however, in agricultural practices and forest protection.

For the most part, big environmental programs in Switzerland are coordinated and overseen by an official agency known as BUWAL, which is a German acronym for the Swiss Federal Agency for the Environment, Forests, and Landscape.

5

Protection of waterways is mandated in the Swiss Federal Constitution.

ENERGY RESOURCES

Energy conservation is a major concern for the Swiss, who have no oil reserves of their own and almost no coal or other fossil fuels. In fact, fossil fuels produce less than 5 percent of Swiss electricity. Even so, the government has set a target to cut fossil fuel use by 20 percent by 2020. Thanks to the country's abundance of powerful rivers and the dams that have been built to harness them, Switzerland produces large amounts of hydroelectric power. Renewable and abundant, water power is often called Switzerland's most important natural resource.

HYDROELECTRIC POWER In 2013 hydroelectric power plants contributed 57.9 percent to Switzerland's overall electricity production. It has about 556 hydropower plants; the largest is the Grande Dixence in the canton of Valais. The dam, on the Dixence River, is the tallest gravity dam in the world. Most of the water comes from glacier melt in the summer. The dam fuels four power stations, generating enough electricity to power 400,000 Swiss households.

NUCLEAR PHASE-OUT In 2013, nuclear power produced 39.3 percent of Switzerland's energy. However, shortly after an earthquake and tsunami destroyed Japan's Fukushima nuclear power facility in 2011, the Swiss government made a radical decision. It committed to the phase out of nuclear power in the country. As power plants reach the end of their useful life, they will be closed and not replaced. No new facilities will be built. In place of nuclear energy, the Swiss intend to create a sustainable energy system by 2050. At present, the country has four active nuclear plants and one that has been decommissioned.

RENEWABLE SOURCES

Although it plays a small role now in the Swiss energy profile, renewable resources are the way of the future. The Swiss are looking to increase their use of solar and wind power and continue to tap their abundant water resources. Through new technology, even municipal waste—mainly household trash—

can be a clean source of energy. About twenty-eight Swiss incineration plants generate enough electricity for 250,000 homes.

POLLUTION

Every country on Earth has pollution problems, even Switzerland. Compared to many nations, Switzerland's environment is in relatively good condition; nevertheless, the Swiss are not being complacent. The government pays close attention to environmental protection.

Switzerland is not immune to the pollution problems caused by motor vehicles. Here, traffic grinds to a halt on the road to Lucerne.

AIR Any country with as many motor vehicles as Switzerland has is bound to have air quality issues. Fine particulate matter in the air is a matter of growing concern. These microscopic particles affect the climate and are also dangerous to human health. They are part of what gets spewed into the air by factory emissions and vehicular exhaust. Air pollution does not respect national boundaries, so some of what affects Switzerland's air is blown in from other countries. The Swiss government is working with the European Union to address these emissions. In addition, the Swiss are looking at how their own driving habits and use of fuel adds to the problem.

In 2012, Parliament approved a revision of the CO2 Act, which stipulates that greenhouse gas emissions in Switzerland be reduced by at least 20 percent by 2020 as compared with 1990 levels.

WATER About 80 percent of Switzerland's drinking water comes from groundwater. The water quality is good, but is subject to contamination by agricultural run-off, pesticides, and fertilizers. Much was accomplished in the second half of the twentieth century to protect the country's lakes and rivers. New sewage treatment plants have improved water quality. However, micropollutants remain a problem, because the treatment plants cannot break them down. The country hopes to install new systems for the elimination of micropollutants in waste water in one hundred water treatment plants.

Just a few years ago, hikers climbing the Trift Glacier in the western Alps could reach the Trift Hut on foot. The hut is run by the Swiss Alpine Club. By 2004, however, the glacier had receded to the point where that was no longer possible. To make the climb accessible again, a pedestrian suspension bridge was built across a deep canyon in 2005. The bridge itself became a tourist attraction, and it was replaced in 2009 with a more permanent structure.

Even getting to the bridge is an adventure. First, a 1.5 mile-long (2.4 km) gondola ride takes people to the remote reaches of the Trift Gorge. From there, a ninety-minute walk on a mountain trail leads to the bridge. The 558-foot (170-m) Trift Bridge is not for the timid! It hangs 328 feet (100 m) above Triftsee (Trift Lake) and the views are breathtaking. The lake itself is new, having been formed by the melting glacier after 2002.

BIODIVERSITY

Switzerland is thought to be a pristine land welcoming to all life forms, but, in fact, 224 species of plants and animals have become extinct in the country over the last 150 years. Today Switzerland maintains a Red List of endangered plants and animals for special protection. The causes for a loss of biodiversity include the rerouting of water, drying up of wetlands, building and road construction, destruction of natural habitats, and intensive land cultivation. Government agencies are focused on biodiversity monitoring and conservation programs.

CLIMATE CHANGE: MELTING GLACIERS

Switzerland has more than a hundred glaciers on its mountainous terrain, and they are important to the environment. However, these huge masses of ice have been shrinking for more than a century, probably due to air pollution and now climate change. Over the last few decades the temperature in Switzerland's—and all of Europe's—higher mountain regions has increased by one degree Celsius (1.8°F). And the warming continues.

One degree doesn't sound like much but it already has had a significant effect on the environment. That small rise in temperature pushes the tree line up by 330 feet (100 m), which in turn changes habitats, leaving some species in the lurch. The warming also causes rock slides and floods as retreating glaciers loosen formerly frozen terrain.

Summer ice melt from the glaciers provides water for the country's major rivers. As the glaciers recede, a lower volume of water will severely impact Switzerland's hydroelectric capacity, though the simultaneous creation of new lakes, which has already happened, might provide other water sources.

Not least, the shrinking glaciers will impact the vitally important Swiss ski resort and tourism businesses.

INTERNET LINKS

www.swissworld.org/en/environment
"Switzerland and the Environment" covers a large number of environmental topics in great detail.

www.spiegel.de/international/europe/melting-glaciers-turning-alps-into-lake-region-a-896729.html
"Land O' Lakes: Melting Glaciers Transform Alpine Landscape" is a look at the climate change situation in the Swiss Alps.

epi.yale.edu/epi/country-profile/switzerland
The Environmental Performance Index shows Switzerland's strongest and weakest sectors.

THE SWISS

A Swiss carriage driver in the resort town of Davos has the look of a robust Swiss mountain man.

WHO ARE THE SWISS? ARE THEY really just Germans, Italians, and French living together in an exclusive club? To an outsider, it can seem that way, but the Swiss themselves would find such an assertion to be insulting. The Swiss people are not Germans, Italians, French, and Romansh; they are Swiss. Switzerland is, as its name makes clear, a confederacy, which means a league or alliance of different groups that have come together for a purpose. That purpose is freedom and independence. Nevertheless, the question of a national identity that transcends linguistic, religious, and cultural differences is still debated. Does such a Swiss identity exist, and if so, what is it?

Switzerland stands at a geographical crossroads where several cultures meet. People of different ethnic origins and languages, the Swiss have found a unique way to coexist and maintain their diversity. Switzerland's federalism incorporates an enormous respect for the cultural differences of its people and a determination to preserve those differences. If a

6

The motto of the Confederation of Switzerland reflects its diverse population: *Unus pro omnibus, omnes pro uno* ("One for all, all for one").

nation can be said to have certain characteristics, the Swiss are conservative, unfussy, prudent, and industrious.

Swiss diversity is limited, however. It is not a racial, ethnic, or religious diversity; the Swiss are overwhelmingly white, Western European, and Christian. Catholics and Protestants live side by side in almost equal numbers. There are also tiny Greek Orthodox and Jewish communities and a growing Muslim population. In 2015, Switzerland had a population of about 8.2 million, including 1.9 million foreign nationals.

THE PEOPLE OF TICINO

Ticino is the part of Switzerland that is closest to Italy. At various times in Switzerland's history it was annexed by Italy. Most of its people speak Italian and are more Mediterranean in look and character.

Ticino is a mountainous canton and historically has been depressed economically. Farmers grew grapes, tobacco, olives, and vegetables to survive. It is the warmest part of Switzerland in the summer, when there are severe thunderstorms that cause the Ticino River to flood much of the

People enjoy eating outdoors on the Ascona promenade at Lake Maggiore in Ticino.

arable land. Winters, however, are relatively mild. The typical Ticino house is a stone-roofed cottage high in the hills. Lakes Maggiore and Lugano occupy a considerable area of the canton. The scenic lakes, mountainous areas, and mild climate fostered a tourism industry after the end of World War II.

This tourism and the increasing wealth of the other cantons have affected the lifestyle of the Ticino people. Many of the old stone-roofed cottages in the mountains have been purchased as summer homes for wealthy Zürich residents. This has increased the local real estate value, often to the dissatisfaction of the residents. In addition many of the local inhabitants have emigrated to the other more prosperous cantons to work.

There have been improvements in the lives of the people who have chosen to stay. Although agriculture is still practiced, Ticino has become a center of tourism and international finance. In the city of Lugano, many people have found work in the service industries.

THE PEOPLE OF GRAUBÜNDEN

The origin of the people who live in this upland region of Switzerland can be traced to the Rhaetians, an ancient people related to the Etruscans in Italy. Thus the people living in Graubünden (or *Grisons*, in French) are of a completely different origin than the Swiss of French and German heritage, and their language has evolved from different sources.

Most Europeans are believed to be of Indo-European origin, but not so the people of Graubünden. The Romansh languages have Etruscan, Semitic, and perhaps Celtic influences on top of the basic Latin imposed by the Romans. Although Graubünden also contains Swiss-German and Italian speakers today, the Romansh language is spoken by about a third of the population, and in that language, the name of the place is *Grischun*. It is the only official trilingual Swiss canton.

Graubünden is Switzerland's largest canton, occupying about 2,743 square miles (7,106 square km) in the southeastern part of the country. The canton got its name from the Gray League (Grauer Bund), which was formed in 1395 with the purpose of restoring peace to the area. The league was so named because most of the members, who were peasants, wore gray clothes.

A hiker crosses a stream in Graubünden.

Graubünden is largely rural. The people practice pastoral agriculture and produce wine, and many of them find employment in the very exclusive winter resorts in the area. Graubünden is also the home of the Swiss National Park, the only national park in Switzerland.

THE PEOPLE OF THE VALAIS

The Valais was a late entrant into the Confederation, joining in 1815 after centuries of exploitation by the French dukes of Savoy and eventually Napoleon's France. For Valais, joining the Confederation was a last resort rather than an achievement.

The Valais is a narrow valley 93 miles (150 km) long, lying between the Valaisian and Bernese alps, and the skyline is dominated by mountains. Extending from the central valley are many smaller valleys that even today are quite inaccessible.

The people of the Valais have always seen themselves as being a bit different from the rest of the Swiss. If a whole group of people can be characterized, they would probably describe themselves as headstrong, self-confident, and very independent. They are largely French-speaking and have a very distinctive accent that any Swiss can recognize after hearing the first few words. In some rural areas a dialect of French is spoken.

The Matterhorn and the nearby resort town of Zermatt attract tourists. Wine production and cattle breeding are still practiced. Each spring the animals are taken to the summer pastures on the mountains and brought down again in the fall.

THE PEOPLE FROM OTHER PLACES

For centuries foreigners have come to Switzerland as a place of refuge. Some very famous people have made Switzerland their home, however temporarily. The nineteenth-century German writers Johann Wolfgang von Goethe and Friedrich von Schiller lived in Switzerland for a time, and Mary Shelley wrote her novel *Frankenstein* in Switzerland. Richard Wagner, the German

"Man is born free, and everywhere he is in chains. Those who think themselves the masters of others are indeed greater slaves than they." —Jean-Jacques Rousseau, The Social Contract, *1762*

Carl Gustav Jung

Claude Nicollier

Switzerland has produced a large number of people who have made important contributions in the arts and sciences. These include mathematicians, scientists, philosophers, and psychologists. Here are a few of the best known Swiss personalities:

Mathematicians: *Leonhard Euler (1707–1783), Daniel Bernoulli (1700–1782), Paul Bernays (1888–1977)*

Psychologists: *Hermann Rorschach (1884–1922), Carl Gustav Jung (1875–1961), founder of analytical psychology; Jean Piaget (1896–1980), pioneer in developmental studies; Elizabeth Kubler-Ross (1926–2004), pioneer in near-death studies.*

Philosophers: *Jean-Jacques Rousseau (1712–1778); Denis de Rougemont (1906–1985)*

Economists: *Leon Walras (1834–1910), J.C.L. Simonde de Sismondi (1773–1842)*

Other scientists: *Ferdinand de Saussure (1857–1913), linguist; Auguste Piccard (1884–1962), physicist; Jacques Piccard (1922–2008), oceanographer; Bertrand Piccard (b. 1958), psychiatrist, balloonist; Claude Nicollier (b. 1944), astronaut, flew on four Space Shuttle missions.*

Humanities: *Henri Dunant (1828–1910), founder of the Red Cross.*

People from the canton Schwyz march in the Swiss National Day Parade in colorful costumes.

There are almost as many different traditional costumes in Switzerland as there are valleys. These costumes, highly regarded and valued, are worn during the many festive occasions in Switzerland. Many costumes display the Swiss craft of embroidery. The most distinctive ones are probably those of the Gruyère region. The armailli (arm-ah-EE-yee), or herdsman, of the Gruyère wears the bredzon (bredd-ZAHNN), a short blue cloth or canvas jacket with sleeves gathered at the shoulders, and edelweiss embroidered on the lapels. The woman's dress from the same region is plain and worn with a red scarf round the neck. For festivals, a silk apron and a long-sleeved jacket are added. The straw hat is edged with velvet and has crocheted ribbons hanging off it.

Women from Saint Gall wear shimmering gold lace caps, while women from Appenzell wear lace caps with spreading wings (right).

Women represent the canton Appenzell in the same parade.

The Appenzell herdsman wears intricate trousers with heavily patterned straps, and suspenders carrying pictures of the cows he tends. He also wears a silver earring on his right ear. In Nidwalden and Obwalden, the woman's dress is ornamented with silver, and a silver comb is worn in the side of the hair. The man's shirt from the same region is heavily embroidered.

composer, left his native Germany and took refuge in Switzerland. Friedrich Nietzsche, who taught at Basel University, got the idea for his work *Thus Spake Zarathustra* while on vacation in Engadine, in Graubünden. German-born Albert Einstein became a Swiss citizen in 1901 and was working in the patent office in Bern when he developed his famous theory of relativity. The great Russian writer Fyodor Dostoyevsky also lived in Switzerland. Russian revolutionaries Vladimir Lenin, Grigory Zinovyev, and Leon Trotsky, Russian composer Igor Stravinsky, and Irish writer James Joyce all waited out at least part of World War I in Switzerland. Joyce spent his final days in Zürich.

Many famous people still find their way to Switzerland, attracted by the banking system and the tax concessions. Wealthy immigrants have also chosen to live in Switzerland because of its stability and high quality of life. There are foreign workers attracted by the good wages, and those who escape from difficult political situations in their home countries.

INTERNET LINKS

www.everyculture.com/Sa-Th/Switzerland.html
This overview Switzerland and its culture includes a good discussion of its people and identity.

www.biography.com/people/groups/swiss
"Famous Swiss People" is a short list with biographies.

www.topswitzerland.ch/swiss_top_people.html
This is another list of significant Swiss people, with some unusual additions.

world4.eu/switzerland-national-folk-costumes-from-1896
"The Swiss national costumes of 17th —19th century originals" is a gallery of images with many links.

LIFESTYLE

A woman enjoys the sunshine as she reads a newspaper at an outdoor cafe.

S WITZERLAND ENJOYS A PRIVILEGED position in the world. This is due, among other things, to its early industrialization and a well-educated population that has enabled the country to specialize in producing high-quality products and providing valuable services, such as banking and investing.

The population consists of people from diverse ethnic and linguistic groups, and the nation has learned to survive as a cohesive unit.

There is no doubt that the Swiss are conscious of both their own wealth and their exemption from the world's major upheavals. More than just a collection of bank managers, clockmakers, and chocolate entrepreneurs, Switzerland has led the world in other important ways, such as in its long tradition of aid and disaster relief work.

LIFE IN THE CITIES

The cities and towns of Switzerland are home to about 73 percent of the population. Each city has its own character, determined by its population mix, its focus as a city, and its architectural heritage. As in other world cities, urban growth and the demand for office buildings in the inner city have meant that large residential areas have grown around the cities. Swiss cities are heavily populated, and commuters on their way to work may spend time waiting in line for buses, streetcars, or a ferryboat.

7

Switzerland is the birthplace of the Red Cross, one of the world's most important humanitarian organizations. The Red Cross flag, a red cross on a white background, is simply a reverse of the flag of Switzerland, showing proud Swiss roots.

A tram drives down the center of Bahnhofstrasse while people walk on the sidewalks in Zurich.

In the cities, sidewalk cafés are one of the focal points of daily life. In summer, they are crowded with workers and tourists having their lunch or watching the world go by. In the French-speaking cities, the people prefer to drink wine with their lunch, while in the German-speaking towns, such as Zürich, beer rivals wine as the popular drink.

Nightlife in the cities begins early, at around 8 p.m. For those who want a night out there is sufficient entertainment to keep them occupied, from restaurants and movie theaters to clubs and bars. The evening's activities end early. By midnight, the restaurants and bars are closed and only the most avant-garde of clubs stay open until 2 or 3 a.m.

In Zürich and other major cities, drugs are a real problem, with some city parks becoming centers for young drug users who have dropped out of mainstream society. Switzerland's pragmatic policy of providing drug addicts with free methadone and clean needles has greatly reduced deaths and cut crime rates. The practice also helps to combat AIDS.

LIFE IN THE COUNTRY

Over the last century, the urbanization of the country has seen large population movements from the countryside into the cities. At the same time, agricultural output has increased by means of mechanization, improved fertilizers, and economies of scale as farms get much larger.

People in the rural cantons of Switzerland have historically been more conservative in their outlook than those living in the cities. Now many of them find work in the tourism industry, which in Switzerland employs them more or less year round. Hotels must be cleaned and the guests catered to, restaurants must provide the tourists with meals, and sports centers and health spas must be kept in efficient running condition.

In Alpine regions such as the Valais, people live in tiny communities that are continually shrinking. As more young people emigrate to the cities, life becomes harder for those left behind, especially since tourism and the desire for country homes has put the price of houses in the countryside out of reach for any poorer person who wishes to live there. The large number of vacation homes also ensures that the winter months are lonely ones for those who live in the countryside all year round. Spring and summer, however, bring lots of visitors and festivals to liven up their days.

A child offers a nibble to a baby goat. City dwellers with vacation homes find country life to be a welcome antidote to the urban scene.

LIFE'S MAJOR EVENTS

The vast majority of the people in Switzerland are Christians, with somewhat more Catholics than Protestants. There are also tiny Jewish, Greek Orthodox, and, more recently, Muslim communities in the country. Like other people, the Swiss celebrate the major events in a person's life, such as birth, marriage, and death.

Birth is celebrated in a quiet ceremony with the family going to church for the baptism. The child's name is decided as a matter of personal taste rather than on any religious grounds. In church, the child is given godparents, who promise to be responsible for the child's religious upbringing. In most cases this is symbolic, although the parents usually choose a close family member or friend.

At age seven, the Catholic child receives instruction on the meaning of Holy Communion, and then in a public ceremony receives the Host with other children of the same age. At age thirteen, both Protestant and Catholic children are confirmed in their religion. Catholic children take an additional Confirmation name at this ceremony, although it is rarely used.

Marriage is still popular in Switzerland, although there are many young people who choose not to observe this ceremony. A church wedding is often followed by a honeymoon abroad. Today many people marry in a civil ceremony and forego the church.

Swiss funerals are quiet affairs. The family attends a funeral service in church, followed by the burial in the local graveyard.

Besides these major events in life, the Swiss observe other cycles. The change in seasons is celebrated each year, especially in rural areas such as the Valais. There, the farmers wait for spring to come so that they can go with the animals to the high pastures, gradually working their way back down the mountain as the grass is eaten. Celebrations take place during this period, with festivals and mock battles between the cows.

The events of the Christian year are also celebrated in much the same way as in other Christian countries. Religious celebrations, both somber and joyous, are observed in accordance with the Christian calendar, the most important ones being Christmas, Easter, and Corpus Christi.

SOCIAL INTERACTION

The Swiss are great consumers of the media. Most cities are connected to cable television and so there are many programs to watch. The Swiss are also avid newspaper readers. Swiss social life revolves around these things and the family. Nightlife, as we have seen, ends early. People work fairly hard—the average work week is 41.7 hours—and at the end of a long day, most people go home to their families. The coffee shops and bars in the cities and villages are meeting places where people can discuss politics or just read their newspapers in companionable silence.

In a society made up of four distinct language groups, at least three religious groups, and many foreigners, the ability to get along with one's neighbors is a desirable quality that has been bred into the Swiss as a way of life. The Swiss are essentially home-loving, careful people, with a high degree of tolerance, great interest in preserving their cultural heritage, and a great sense of civic duty. They appreciate the benefits of their country's neutrality and the wealth that a public-spirited workforce can bring. There are very few strikes among workers in Switzerland. The Swiss have learned that all differences can be negotiated rather than fought out in public. Since 1937 there has been a regularly renewed agreement between employers and workers to settle their disputes peacefully.

THE ROLE OF WOMEN

Switzerland is by its own admission a conservative country. In a country that values democracy so highly, it is strange that women did not get the right to vote in federal elections until 1971. One demicanton, Appenzell Inner Rhodes, denied women this right for almost twenty more years, with various referenda to change the law failing. Finally, in 1991 the Swiss high court ordered Appenzell Inner Rhodes to join the rest of Switzerland and allow women the right to vote.

On paper, women have had the right to equal pay since 1981, although they are still underrepresented in many areas, particularly in politics. In fact, an official study early this century found that women in Switzerland generally earn 21.5 percent less than their male counterparts, although this earnings gap had been shrinking throughout the previous decade.

Ruth Dreifuss helped pave the way for women in Swiss politics.

In 1984 Elisabeth Kopp became the first woman to be elected to the seven-person Federal Council, but she resigned before her term of office ended over a political scandal of which she was later cleared. Trade union leader Christiane Brunner campaigned for a seat on the Federal Council in 1993 but was denied after she had a smear campaign directed against her. Ruth Dreifuss was the second woman to be elected to the Federal Council in 1993 and became Switzerland's first female president in 1999. Another woman, Ruth Metzler, gained a seat in the Federal Council in 1999. Metzler's entry into the Council was notable not only because of her gender but also because of her youth. She was only thirty-four years old at the time of her appointment. In 1971, women made up only 5 percent of parliament. In 2015, they held 31 percent of the seats.

SOCIAL STRUCTURES

Switzerland is a welfare state, meaning that as part of its duties the state provides all its citizens with generously subsidized health care, pensions, maternity benefits, and education. These benefits are paid for on the federal level using money that workers contribute to a compulsory national insurance fund; they can draw on this fund in their old age or when sick. At the cantonal level, each canton provides funds and services to the destitute or needy. At the commune level, additional funds are allowed for individual needs. This explains why every Swiss resident must be a member of a commune and remains a member of that commune unless he or she applies to join another. It is ultimately the responsibility of the commune to look after its needy.

EDUCATION

In Switzerland, each canton is responsible for drawing up its own curriculum, school materials, and teacher-training program for primary, middle, and advanced school education. There are twenty-six different educational systems operating in Switzerland, one in each canton. The cantons must meet federal standards, but beyond that each canton is autonomous.

Federal regulations determine that children start school at age six or seven and continue for eight years. In some cantons, an optional ninth year

A nine-year-old works on his assignment in his classroom in Moudon, in western Switzerland.

has been introduced, and all the cantons offer two optional preschool years of kindergarten. Most children attend preschool for one or two years at age five or six. After that, there are between four to six years of primary school, depending on the canton, and three to five years of secondary school. Thus in some cantons, children go to secondary school at age ten, while in others, they move to secondary school at age twelve.

At the secondary level, children are streamed; that is, they are put into different schools depending on their ability. One category of secondary school offers four years of apprenticeship training leading to a craft or trade of some kind; another offers academic education, where children are prepared for university or an institute of technology; while the third offers vocational training, which is conducted in collaboration with private companies. Each canton arranges the training of apprentices. Students study part-time and spend a large proportion of their day in the work-place learning their trade. Higher vocational training in colleges trains students to become engineers, managers, economists, or social workers.

The Swiss education system has its drawbacks, since at the time they enter secondary school children are still young and either do not always know what they want or have not yet reached their full potential. The system is being reviewed so that streaming is delayed, to give young people more time to develop and gain a well-rounded education.

NATIONAL DEFENSE

For a neutral country, Switzerland spends a great deal of money on national defense—around the same amount it spends on social welfare.

Switzerland has almost 135,000 people on active duty, of which 4,230 are professionals, with the rest being conscripts or volunteers. The state considers that each man's military obligation is just as important as his civic ones. Thus part of every Swiss man's life is devoted to his military duties.

At age twenty, all Swiss men are required to attend a seventeen-week training session where they learn the basics and are given their equipment. This equipment, including weapons, ammunition, gas mask, and uniform, is kept at home and soldiers are responsible for maintaining it. Between ages

Swiss teachers are well paid, compared to teachers in many other countries. In 2010, the average salary of a teacher in Switzerland was $112,000 per year. For comparison, the average teacher salary in the United States was $58,260.

THE RED CROSS

Jean-Henri Dunant (1828–1910) had no intention of being a world benefactor. He was as interested as any other Swiss in setting up a business for himself, and to that end he went to Algeria, where he began to trade in grain. But things went wrong. The money he borrowed in Switzerland to start his operation could not be repaid, and so he decided to enlist help from Napoleon III. He followed Napoleon to the Battle of Solferino (1859) in northern Italy, where he accidentally witnessed the terrible casualties that the battle caused. He spent two days personally helping the injured and then returned to Switzerland with a lot more on his mind than grain.

In 1862 Dunant toured Switzerland and wrote an account of what he had witnessed. He proposed that armies of all nations should have trained non-combatant volunteers to provide help to the wounded of both sides of any battle. He also suggested the need for international treaties to guarantee the protection of the combatants. His actions brought about the signing of the first Geneva Convention. In 1863, the Red Cross was formed in Geneva under the leadership of Gustave Moynier, who eventually forced Dunant out of the organization. Being more of an idealist than a businessman, Dunant found himself bankrupt and went into hiding to escape his creditors. He lived in poverty in various cities and villages and was mostly forgotten. He got his reward, however, when he received the Nobel Peace Prize in 1901— the very first one.

Today, there are Red Cross and Red Crescent societies in almost every country, with more than ninety million members, volunteers and staff. The headquarters of the International Red Cross is located in Geneva and is staffed by Swiss citizens. Switzerland is the guardian of the four Geneva Conventions regarding prisoners of war, the wounded, and refugees.

twenty and thirty-two, men attend eight three-week retraining courses. Between ages thirty-three and forty-two, they are put in the military reserve and attend three two-week courses. After age forty-three and until age fifty, they are still reserve soldiers but are only required to perform one week of training per year. In total, military training takes up about a year and a half of a man's life, more for officers. Women may volunteer for military training. Women make up less than 1 percent of the total, but 25 percent of the career soldiers.

Switzerland's total military manpower stands at about 1.9 million. In 2012 the country's military expenditure was $4.83 billion. The country has tanks, jet fighters, canons, and missiles. In addition, there are camouflaged underground storage caverns and military bases, all of them designed to withstand nuclear blasts.

Other underground storage spaces hold medicine, repair shops for military machinery, and food. For the civilians, there are also underground shelters capable of withstanding heavy bombing. In the early 1970s a government-mandated program to provide people with bomb shelters was inaugurated. Today Switzerland boasts pretty close to a readily available place in a shelter for every resident.

A Swiss soldier stands at attention in front of the Swiss flag in Bern.

INTERNET LINKS

www.huffingtonpost.com/2013/10/07/switzerland_0_n_4038031.html
"Why Switzerland Has Some of the Happiest, Healthiest Citizens in the World" is a look at the Swiss lifestyle.

www.historytoday.com/richard-cavendish/founding-red-cross-movement
History Today offers a short article on "The Founding of the Red Cross Movement."

www.swissinfo.ch/eng/switzerland-how-to/daily-life
Information on daily life in Switzerland can be found here.

RELIGION

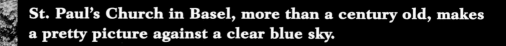

St. Paul's Church in Basel, more than a century old, makes a pretty picture against a clear blue sky.

CHRISTIANITY FIRST CAME TO Switzerland through the Roman merchants and soldiers. However, it was not until the early Middle Ages, in the seventh century and quite late in the history of Christianity, that the bulk of the Swiss population was converted. This final conversion was due to the work of a group of traveling missionaries, led by Saint Columban and Saint Gall or Gallus, two dedicated and devout Irish monks. They found an ancient Celtic religion in Switzerland and hurled into the lakes the graven images of the pagan religion.

In the sixteenth century, Catholic Switzerland was racked by the Reformation, when the new Protestants tried to take political power in Zürich. This led to war between the Protestant and the Catholic states. Switzerland, like the rest of Europe, was divided along religious lines.

Those divisions again became inflamed in the nineteenth century, when Lucerne, a predominantly Catholic canton, decided to put its school system under the control of the Jesuits. Protestant groups attacked the city, and the seven Catholic cantons decided to secede from the Confederation. The Sonderbund civil war followed. The dispute

A Protestant celebration

led to the Swiss Constitution of 1848, which among other things, declared complete religious tolerance, with the exception of the Jesuits, who were banned from Switzerland. This ban was officially lifted only in 1973.

The importance of religious tolerance has remained to this day. The once clear divisions of cantons into Catholic and Protestant camps have softened since the Industrial Revolution, when large numbers of people from the rural cantons moved to the cities. Now the Catholic areas are mainly the southern Italian-speaking ones as well as those in central Switzerland. The French-speaking areas, and the areas to the north and east, are largely Protestant. Nationally, roughly 38.2 percent are Catholics, while 26.9 percent are Protestant. Muslims make up nearly 5 percent, while people of other religions, or no religion, account for the rest.

PROTESTANTISM

During the Reformation, the two main centers of Protestantism in Switzerland were Zürich, under the influence of Huldrych Zwingli, and Geneva, under the influence of John Calvin. Zürich was and is mostly German-speaking; Geneva is largely French-speaking. Later, Vaud, the canton north of Geneva, and Neuchâtel, its neighbor, were converted. Bern, the largest canton in central Switzerland, also joined the Reformation. As time passed and the citizens of the cantons moved about within the Federation, each city developed a character of its own but had a mixed community of Protestants and Catholics. The numerous Protestant groups formed the Federation of Swiss Evangelical Churches.

In its early stages, Protestantism in Switzerland was a fiercely puritan religion, disapproving of all frivolity and excess. This can still be seen in the

This Benedictine abbey in northeastern Switzerland was founded in 934 on the site of the hermitage of Saint Meinrad. Huldrych Zwingli, the religious reformer, was the parish priest from 1516 to 1518.

The abbots of the monastery were very powerful. Even when they had lost most of their power after 1789, the abbey remained a major place of pilgrimage for Europeans, who visited the Black Madonna statue. The abbey also has a library containing rare and beautiful manuscripts. To house all the pilgrims, a baroque-style church was built in the eighteenth century. The buildings and grounds of the church and abbey are very beautiful and remain a major tourist attraction.

Protestant churches of Switzerland, which are simple, austere, and bare compared to the Catholic churches with their highly elaborate artwork, decoration, and artifacts.

Calvinism, the basis of modern Swiss Protestantism, began as a rejection of some of the tenets of the Church of Rome. It rejected the role of the Pope as God's representative and instead declared that all people could petition directly to God. It refused to accept any doctrine beyond those laid down in the Bible, so that the Catholic belief in transubstantiation (the changing of the bread and wine into the body and blood of Christ) was rejected. The ornate decoration of the older churches was thrown out, as was much of the ceremony. More importantly, perhaps, Calvinists believe in predestination—the idea that a soul's eventual destiny, especially its place in heaven or hell, is foreordained by God.

Today, Protestant churches are managed in each canton by a synod, a body of lay persons who decide on church matters. Swiss Protestants celebrate the same religious events as Catholics. Christmas, Easter, and Lent figure largely in their religious calendar and are celebrated in very similar ways.

ROMAN CATHOLICISM

Enthusiastic Catholic teens wave to Pope John Paul II during his visit to Bern in 2004.

Roman Catholics form the largest religious group in Switzerland. During the Reformation, the rural cantons and the cantons in central Switzerland were not affected by the new ideas of Calvin and Zwingli. Those states now make up the predominantly Catholic areas.

The Roman Catholic and Protestant churches in Switzerland share a belief in the same God. Their differences are in matters of doctrine and government. The chief differences between the two religions are that Catholics believe in confession and absolution, and revere Mary, the mother of Jesus, in the belief that she will intercede on behalf of the repentant. Protestants do not accept these doctrines. The government of the Catholic Church is less democratic. Ultimate power lies with the Pope in Rome, and each diocese in a country is governed by a bishop.

Like Protestants, Roman Catholics celebrate the main events of the Christian calendar. Christmas is a public holiday in Switzerland, but for both sects it is a private family affair, with little public activity on the two days of the holiday. Catholic and Protestant children both celebrate Saint Nicholas' Day on December 6. Gifts are given, and in some areas, particularly in Graubünden, large and noisy parades take place. On Christmas Eve, Catholic families attend midnight Mass together.

Later in the year, Lent, a period of penitence and fasting, is observed, marking the forty days that Christ spent in the wilderness. All public festivals are avoided, and people give up some luxury for the duration. On Easter Sunday, the Resurrection of Christ is celebrated.

The feast of Corpus Christi falls in late May or early June every year; it is a special celebration of the Eucharist, which has been observed since 1264. Several towns have parades, with each area stressing different themes in their costumes.

In Mendrisio, a town in the Italian part of Switzerland, congregants perform a passion play at Easter time.

SAINT GALL AND HIS ABBEY

There has been a monastery of some sort at Saint Gallen in eastern Switzerland since the traveling Irish monk Gall (550–646) built a sleeping cell and a wooden church there in the seventh century. Gall was one of the twelve people who accompanied Saint Columban on his mission from Ireland to spread Christianity throughout continental Europe. During the Middle Ages, the town of Saint Gallen became an enormously powerful ecclesiastical center. In the eighteenth century, the monastery and its lands were taken by the French. The monastery became a cathedral in 1847.

The Saint Gallen Cathedral represents many different eras of architectural history, with eighth-century buildings and a Collegiate Church dating back to the eighteenth century. The most beautiful room in this complex of buildings is the eighteenth-century abbey library, with its elaborate plasterwork and paintings. It contains some very rare manuscripts, including Irish examples dating back to the period between the seventh and twelfth centuries.

The Abbey precinct of St. Gallen, including the cathedral and the Abbey Library, is listed as a UNESCO World Heritage Site.

OTHER GROUPS

Besides the Roman Catholic Church, there is another Catholic diocese in Switzerland not associated with it. This is the Old Catholic Church. Differing slightly on matters of doctrine, the group is represented mostly in Bern.

Switzerland's need of foreign workers and the huge tide of refugees moving around Europe in the 1980s and 1990s has brought other religions, such as Islam, to Switzerland. After Christianity, Islam is now the second largest religion in the country. Muslims now make up 4.9 percent of the population.

The Jewish presence in the country is very small, numbering about 17,500 people. A historic pattern of discrimination, heightened during the Holocaust when most European Jewish refugees fleeing persecution were forbidden entry to the country, is a significant reason for this.

INTERNET LINKS

www.expatica.com/ch/insider-views/Swissworld-Religion-in-Switzerland_107839.html
"Swissworld: Religion in Switzerland" offers a good overview of the topic.

www.historylearningsite.co.uk/John_Calvin.htm
The History Learning Site offers an in-depth biography of John Calvin and his influence.

www.myswitzerland.com/en-us/benedictine-abbey-with-the-lady-chapel-with-the-black-madonna.html
Watch the video on this site about the Einsiedeln monastery and the town.

www.swissinfo.ch/eng/empty-pews_one-in-four-shuns-religion-in-switzerland/29877728
"One in four shuns religion in Switzerland" is on the SWI swissinfo site.

LANGUAGE

gesperrt

barrée

chiusa

closed

Three of the languages pictured on this ski slope sign are official languages of Switzerland. Which one is not?

9

I T'S RATHER SURPRISING THAT Switzerland exists at all. For such a small country to be divided into four language regions—with language diversity even within those regions—it would seem the center could not hold. Language is a powerful common denominator, and history has shown that people will often align with others who speak the same language.

The international abbreviation for Switzerland is CH, which comes from its Latin name, *Confoederatio Helvetica*.

German
French
Italian
Romansh

This map shows the four language regions of Switzerland.

A campaign poster for an initiative relating to gold reserves urges a "yes" vote in French.

In Switzerland's case, one might therefore expect the French-speaking region to become part of France, the Italian-speaking region to become part of Italy, and so on. But that hasn't happened in more than seven hundred years, and probably never will. The Swiss have figured out how to hold together as a nation despite their different tongues.

Switzerland sits at the very point where three other major cultural regions meet. But its mountainous landscape has meant that whole communities have remained separated and isolated for generations. Consequently, it has four national languages and many regional variations so strong that, in some cases, people speaking dialects of the same language cannot understand one another.

Approximately 64.9 percent of the country speaks some variant of Swiss-German as their mother tongue, 22.6 percent French, 8.3 percent Italian, 0.5 percent Romansh. Another 21 percent speak some other language. (The total exceeds 100 percent because some people speak more than one language.) The last group consists of foreign workers who come from Spain, Portugal, or elsewhere. As with the religious makeup of the country, the language groups are not as clearly defined by geography as they once were. Communities of each language group live in all the cities.

NATIONAL AND OFFICIAL LANGUAGES

Switzerland has problems when standard items like official documents, banknotes, or street signs have to be understood by all its citizens. Switzerland has alleviated this problem to a certain extent by having three official languages: German, French, and Italian. All banknotes and official documents are written in all three languages. In addition, Romansh was made a national language in 1938 and was later accorded the status of semiofficial language in a 1996 referendum. Romansh appears on official documents that are used in Romansh areas, and it is always the formal form of address in areas where the language is spoken.

GERMAN AND SWISS GERMAN

The German spoken in Switzerland evolved separately from the High German used as the standard language in Germany. The Swiss German grammatical structure, vocabulary, and pronunciation are often quite different from Germany's. In addition, Swiss German has three main dialect groups, and subdialects found in isolated valleys and enclaves, so it's not always possible for speakers of different German dialects to understand each other.

However, High German is the official written language used in business and government in Swiss-German-speaking cantons. When necessary, Swiss-German speakers can usually revert to High German, albeit spoken with a Swiss accent. This is because most Swiss-German speakers understand it, read it in books and newspapers, and listen to it on television. News broadcasts are made in standard German, but the sports commentaries are usually in Swiss-German.

The same campaign poster that is on the facing page is shown here in German.

FRENCH

About 22.6 percent of the population of Switzerland speak French, mostly in the west of Switzerland, in the cantons of Geneva, Vaud, and Neuchâtel. With French the situation is a little less complicated than with the other language groups, since there are fewer surviving dialects. Until recent years there were areas, especially around the Valais and Jura, where a dialect of French similar to Savoyard was spoken. Today, only the older people know this dialect, and it is rarely spoken.

ITALIAN AND ITS VARIATIONS

Italian is the official language of Ticino and parts of Graubünden, both relatively small areas of Switzerland. But even within such small communities, there are many different dialects of Italian spoken. Italian dialects are more

A traffic sign written in Romansh language is seen in the tiny village of Zuoz in the canton of Graubuenden.

mutually incomprehensible than German dialects, and there are many different dialects, some more like Lombard (a northern Italian dialect) and others closer to Romansh. The situation is complicated by the fact that even within small villages there are also Romansh and German speakers. The official form is standard Italian, used in conversations of an official nature, as well as in documents and on television. Within the same conversation, two speakers may switch between standard Italian and their common dialect as their discussion shifts between official business and more general matters.

ROMANSH

Although Romansh is spoken only by 0.5 percent of the population in Switzerland, it is one of the country's national languages and is a semi-official language. Romansh's regional center is in Coira, in the Graubünden canton. The language emerged from a combination of the languages spoken in the area before the Roman invasion and the Latin of the Roman Empire. Linguistic scholars believe the Romansh language evolved from the Etruscans, a highly sophisticated society from west-central Italy that flourished before the Roman Empire. Romansh is thought, too, to have influences from an even older Celtic language, as well as from Semitic.

As a result of the historic isolation of small communities in this area, there are five regional dialects of Romansh in Switzerland, each with its own standardized written form. The most widely spoken is the Sursilvan dialect. In the Engadine area of Graubünden, another dialect known as Ladin is spoken, and in central Graubünden, two dialects, Surmiran and Sutsilvan, are spoken. Romansh is also spoken in southern Tyrol in Austria.

Today all of the Romansh-speaking areas have German-speaking or Italian-speaking majorities. As schools standardize languages and television dominates life, maintaining every single dialect as a living language becomes harder with each generation. The fact that there are so many different versions of Romansh makes the survival of the language even less likely. The younger generation of Swiss writers from the Graubünden has in recent decades been developing a steadily growing interest in writing fiction in Romansh. One of the more renowned writers of fiction was Flurin Spescha (1958—2000). Public efforts toward the promotion of trilinguism, a Romansh press, and television and radio broadcasts in Romansh have resulted in an increased interest in preserving and maintaining the tradition of communication and literary practices in the language.

WHAT'S IN A NAME?

With four national languages, giving things a name that everyone understands can be a difficult activity. Even the major cities are called by different names, depending on what region of Switzerland you are in. The name of the country itself varies according to its languages, being known as *Schweiz* (German), *Suisse* (French), *Svizzera* (Italian), and *Svizra* (Romansh). The lakes have different names altogether, depending on which language you use. For instance, that lake that we call Lake Geneva is known to German-speakers as *Genfersee* and to French speakers as *Lac Léman*.

INTERNET LINKS

www.swissvistas.com/languages-spoken-in-switzerland.html#. VRq6KfnF9eY
This page about Swiss languages has good information, a map, and some interesting videos.

www.swissinfo.ch/eng/languages/29177618
This site offers an overview of the Swiss language situation and links to related stories.

www.omniglot.com/writing/romansh.htm
Omniglot is a solid introduction to the Romansh language and written form.

ARTS

This sculpture is a favorite display at the Alimentarium Museum in Vevey. The museum was opened by the Nestle Foundation.

10

W HEN PEOPLE THINK OF THE great arts-producing nations of Europe, they usually think of France, Italy, Germany, or Spain. Rarely do they think of Switzerland. In a famous quote from the movie *The Third Man* (1949), the main character Harry Lime cynically observes, "Like the fella says, in Italy for thirty years under the Borgias they had warfare, terror, murder, and bloodshed, but they produced Michelangelo, Leonardo da Vinci, and the Renaissance. In Switzerland they had brotherly love—they had five hundred years of democracy and peace—and what did that produce? The cuckoo clock."

Of course that isn't true, but it does speak to a perception of Switzerland as a safe but bland place. Switzerland is a small country set in the middle of Europe, so it makes sense that Swiss artists might leave their country to study and work. For that reason, they have long soaked up the influences of a more international art scene, and are therefore sometimes not thought of as Swiss at all. Part of Switzerland's image

In 2014, Switzerland's Bern Art Museum agreed to accept hundreds of artworks bequeathed by the German Nazi-era art hoarder Cornelius Gurlitt. The son of Adolf Hitler's art dealer, Gurlitt was found in 2012 to be hiding some 1,280 works of art, including works by Picasso and Monet. As some of the works are known to have been looted from Holocaust victims, the museum promised not to accept any of those pieces.

Lake Geneva from Chexbres **was painted by Ferdinand Hodler in 1905.**

problem is caused by its three major languages. Because Swiss writers use French, German, or Italian, they become part of the school of literature of France, Germany, or Italy rather than of Switzerland itself.

It's the same for other fields of artistic endeavor. Many famous Swiss personalities, such as the architect Le Corbusier or the painter and sculptor Alberto Giacometti, are considered French or Italian, despite the fact that they were Swiss-born.

Today, Swiss artists are just as likely to consider themselves international artists, as the art scene knows no borders. Nevertheless, this small country has produced some of Europe's most famous artists, and the country boasts some of its most renowned art museums.

FINE ARTS

Ferdinand Hodler (1853—1918) is considered the father of Swiss landscape painting and did his best work at the turn of the century. He also produced many frescoes depicting events in Swiss history, and was also a master at portraiture. In the twentieth century, the painter Giovanni Giacometti developed a Postimpressionist style, while his cousin Augusto Giacometti used colors in an innovative way in his landscape paintings. Félix Vallotton created his own distinctive style of painting—a very bold realism. The famous architect Le Corbusier was also Swiss, although few of his designs can be found in Switzerland. He is also famous for his paintings and, with French artist Amédée Ozenfant, created a new school of art called Purism.

The famous Dada art movement emerged from post-World War I Zürich. The name, chosen at random from a French-German dictionary, is a French word meaning hobby horse. The Dadaists challenged the established rules of art and used shock tactics to make people think differently about art. There were only a few Swiss artists in the group, but they—especially Jean Arp—

"A line is a dot that went for a walk."
—Paul Klee, Swiss artist (1879–1940)

PAUL KLEE, BELATEDLY SWISS ARTIST

Perhaps the most famous Swiss artist of all is Paul Klee (1879–1940). He was born to a Swiss mother and a German father, but grew up in Switzerland. Nevertheless, laws at the time determined citizenship according to the nationality of the father, and Klee was considered German, despite being born and raised in Switzerland.

He studied art in Munich and later settled in Germany, forming part of the Der Blaue Reiter ("The Blue Rider") group. That association of artists rejected commonly held art standards and traditions, and experimented with new forms of visual expression. He taught at the Bauhaus, a famous German design school. Some of his work is completely abstract, while others combine geometric forms with images of animals and people. Many of his paintings were confiscated by the Nazis and declared "degenerate art."

In 1932, during the rise of Fascism in Germany, Klee returned to Switzerland, where he continued to paint. Klee's work is often whimsical and childlike, without being childish, such as in his well-known abstract, Twittering Machine (1922). That small watercolor is now at the Museum of Modern Art in New York. Some of his work reveals mystical or fantastical qualities. Later in his life, as World War II was breaking out, Klee's work reflected more somber concerns. At that point, he was also dying of a chronic illness, and death and angels became common images in his paintings.

Klee applied for Swiss citizenship, but Swiss authorities were in no hurry to claim him as one of their own; they considered his art too revolutionary. Klee died in 1940 at age sixty before his application was processed. Citizenship was granted six days after he died in the country of his birth. Today Klee is recognized as one of the most important artists of the twentieth century.

One of the "Moonrise" sculptures by Ugo Rondinone graces a plaza in San Francisco.

were important members of the movement. Apart from Zürich, Dadaism also flourished in cities abroad, such as New York City, Paris, Berlin, Cologne, and Hannover.

Today's Swiss artists are exploring dynamic new ideas. Swiss-born Ugo Rondinone (b. 1964) is a painter and mixed-media sculptor who creates enigmatic installation pieces. He lives and works in New York City.

Like his compatriot, Urs Fischer (b. 1973) is also a Swiss-born sculptor living in New York. His work is widely varied, and includes room-sized installations, larger-than-life outdoor forms, large painted panels, and small 3D pieces. Many of them feature surprising combinations of everyday objects. Pipilotti Rist (b. 1962) is another Swiss artist who has won international acclaim. She works with video, film, and projected moving images.

In 2015, the celebrated Swiss artist Hans Erni died at age 106. He worked until nearly the end of his long life, producing murals, tapestries, mosaics, sculptures, stained glass windows, and ceramics, as well as posters and book illustrations. In 2009, at the age of 100, he completed a ceramic fresco that decorates the entrance to the United Nations in Geneva.

ARCHITECTURE

One way of tracing the developments in Swiss architectural styles is through the religious buildings. The earliest style found in Switzerland is the Romanesque. Churches in this style were built in the Middle Ages. In Switzerland, the style is characterized by either barrel-vaulted ceilings (rounded tunnel-type ceilings) or by flat-ceilinged bare rooms supported by pillars. The All Saints Benedictine Abbey in Schaffhausen dates from 1106 and is an example of the Romanesque style. Later, this simple design was replaced by the Gothic style. The vaulted ceiling became more complex, and highly ornate altars, as well as heavily carved and ornamented furniture, began to make an appearance. There are many Gothic churches throughout Graubünden and in the German-speaking parts of Switzerland.

From the seventeenth century, a complex, highly ornate new style called Baroque emerged. The Counter-Reformation had begun, and many cantons that had converted to Protestantism were returning to Catholicism and its elaborate church design. Walls were covered in frescoes and paintings. Gilded and carved screens filled the interiors, and paintings of the Virgin Mary and the saints appeared. Elaborate baroque churches can be found in Einsiedeln and Saint Gall. St. Ursen (or Ursus) Cathedral in Solothurn in an important example, dating from 1773.

The Villa Savoye in Poissy, on the outskirts of Paris, is one of the iconic buildings by Le Corbusier. He built it with his cousin Pierre Jeannerette between 1928 and 1931 as a country retreat for the Savoye family. It is now owned by the French government and is open to visitors year round.

In contrast, the modern architectural style is stark and uses reinforced concrete to good effect. An example of this style is the Church of Saint Anthony in Basel designed by Karl Moser.

The most famous Swiss architect is Le Corbusier. He did most of his work in Paris and, later, in Germany. Le Corbusier developed a theory of the relationship between modern machine forms and architectural technique. His buildings are typically raised on stilts. He planned areas of the cities of Algiers, Buenos Aires, and Chandigarh, and his influence can be seen in city planning and architecture all over the world.

PRINTING

Swiss craftsmanship and artistry meet in Swiss printing. Since the Reformation, the Swiss have led in this area. In the sixteenth century Hans Holbein, Niklaus Manuel, and Tobias Stimmer began a tradition of drawing and printmaking by engraving wood that was then inked and printed. The cut grooves in the wood came out clear on paper while the uncut surfaces created the design or picture.

This technique continued until the nineteenth century, when the engraving plates were made of copper with a steel coating. Jean Arp, one of the original Dada artists, produced engravings, as did Marc Chagall, the Russian painter and designer, and Henry Moore, the English sculptor and graphic artist.

FOLK ART

In a country with as strong a rural tradition as Switzerland, it figures that there should be strong and vibrant folk art. This can be seen in many of Switzerland's folk museums, which display the carved and painted farming implements used for the traditional journey to the high pastures in spring.

More characteristic are the *Sennenstreifen* (sen-nen-SCHTRY-fen), long strips of paper or wood painted in a primitive style showing the movement of cattle to the high pastures. The pictures often show long lines of cattle, mountains, farm buildings, and herdsmen in traditional costume. These painted strips were hung over the door to the cowshed or even in the living room. In eastern Switzerland the tradition was for *Senntum-Tafelbilder* (sen-toom TAHH-fell-bill-dare). These are small paintings of similar motifs usually executed in watercolors on cardboard or paper.

Scherenschnitte is a Swiss-German art of cut paper designs. The artists work with tiny, very sharp scissors to create intricate designs which are often, but not always, symmetrical

A craftsperson makes meticulous cuts to a piece of scherenschnitte art.

CUCKOO CLOCKS

One of the best-known symbols of Switzerland is the folksy cuckoo clock. Typically, the wall-hung mechanical clock features a decorated chalet, or mountain house, with little doors. When the clock strikes the hour—and often the half-and quarter-hour as well—the doors open and little figurines appear, sometimes to a music box accompaniment. "Edelweiss" and "Der fröhliche Wanderer" ("The Happy Wanderer") are popular tunes.

Most importantly, out pops a charming carved bird which calls "Cuckoo! Cuckoo!" The weight-driven clockworks are often made with weights shaped like pinecones.

Curiously, despite being associated with Switzerland, cuckoo clocks originated in neighboring Germany, in the Black Forest region, in the eighteenth century. (The idea of having a mechanical cuckoo bird announce the time apparently predates the Black Forest clocks, but the region is generally acknowledged as the birthplace of the clocks as we know them.)

So how did Switzerland get into the act? The addition of the little house, called the chalet style, was a Swiss contribution, added sometime in the 1850s. Today the Lötscher company, based near Zurich, is the only company producing authentic Swiss cuckoo clocks.

Along with being a popular souvenir of Switzerland and the Black Forest, the cuckoo clock has become a kind of cultural icon. As a symbol of passing time, childhood, innocence, and even suspense and foreboding, the clock plays a role in many of the arts. Cuckoo clocks are featured in a surprising number of stories, poems, musical compositions and songs, movies, animations, and TV shows.

Yodeling, a form of singing which involves rapid changes of pitch between high and low, is one of those iconic things that people associate with Switzerland. Of course, all Swiss do

not yodel, but the technique most likely originated there in the Central Alps. Goat or sheep herders in the mountains probably used the distinctive yell, "yod-el-ay-EE-Oooo!" to call their herds.

Yodeling became an important feature of folk music in Switzerland, Austria, and southern Germany. Yodeling figures in other kinds and nationalities of music; for example, it's an important feature of American cowboy country music. But the Swiss style is distinctive to the alpine regions. Today the Swiss hold yodeling festivals, which often include other forms of folk music and instruments.

Early Swiss folk music was often performed by itinerant troupes playing tradition instruments such as the alphorn, hammered dulcimer, fife, hurdy-gurdy, castanets, rebec (a sort of ancient violin), bagpipe, cittern (a sort of ancient guitar) and shawm (an ancient woodwind). After the invention of the accordion in Vienna in 1829, it quickly became a favorite instrument in Swiss folk music.

LITERATURE

With four national languages and a host of dialects, Switzerland has a varied and interesting literary history. As a neutral and safe state, Switzerland also has been home to many non-native people who wrote in the Swiss languages.

Switzerland can claim some famous names in literature. Jean-Jacques

Rousseau was born in Geneva and spent most of his life there until 1742, when he went to live in Paris and became famous. Hermann Hesse was born in Germany but spent most of his life in Switzerland, where he wrote his major works, *Siddhartha*, *Steppenwolf*, and *The Glass Bead Game*, also called *Magister Ludi*. While living in Switzerland he was awarded the Nobel Prize for Literature in 1946.

In the second half of the twentieth century, two Swiss playwrights writing in German became world-renowned for their works that portrayed Swiss society as restricting and complacent. Max Frisch's major works, mainly written after 1945, were influenced by the years he spent living in an isolated and neutral Switzerland during World War II. Friedrich Dürrenmatt's plays include *The Visit*, which has become a modern classic of world drama. Dürrenmatt's many works challenge qualities he saw in Swiss society. Dürrenmatt died in 1990, and Frisch, a year later.

Writing in French in modern times are novelists and poets such as Gustave Roud, Blaise Cendrars, Corinna Bille, and Monique Saint-Hélier. Italian-Swiss writers have also become famous throughout Europe, notably Felice Filippini. Giovanni Orelli, Fabio Pusterla, and Grytzko Mascioni have also made their mark. The situation for Romansh literature is more complex as it has five dialects. It did, however, flourish in the nineteenth century. Noted writers include Cla Biert, Flurin Darms, and Tina Nolfi.

FILM

The small Swiss movie industry has blossomed, producing successful international movies such as Alain Tanner's *Années Lumières* ("*The Light Years*"), which won the Jury Prize at the Cannes Film Festival in 1981. In German, the critically acclaimed movies have been documentaries, while in French, fiction has dominated. In 1991, Xavier Koller's movie *Reise der Hoffnung* ("*Journey of Hope*") won an Oscar. The movie depicted the problems of the enormous number of refugees flooding Europe. The fate of refugees is also highlighted in Joakim Demmer's *Tarifa Traffic*, which was released in 2003. The movie depicts the dangerous and often tragic sea journey that African immigrants make to cross into Europe.

"(Switzerland is) small, and like everything within it, so clean that you can hardly breathe for hygiene, and oppressive precisely because everything is right, fitting, and respectable.... Everything in this country is of an oppressive adequacy."
—Max Frisch (1911–1991), Swiss playwright and novelist

HEIDI, THE GIRL FROM THE ALPS

Canada has Anne Shirley (Anne of Green Gables), England has Mary Lennox (The Secret Garden), Sweden has Pippi Longstocking,* America has Little Orphan Annie—and Switzerland has Heidi. These beloved stories about good-hearted orphan girls have been passed from generation to generation. Heidi, written in 1880 by the Swiss author Johanna Spyri, is the oldest of these.

In the story, young orphaned Heidi is sent to live with her grandfather in the Swiss Alps. He is a bitter old man who lives in seclusion on a mountainside. Cheerful Heidi makes friends with Peter, a young goatherd, and other mountain residents, and eventually wins over her stern grandfather. A few years later, Heidi is sent to work in the city as a hired companion to a wealthy invalid girl named Clara. Although Heidi and Clara become friends, city life in the strict household proves to be unhealthy for the girl she longs for her mountain home. In the end, healthy Alpine air and fresh goat milk restore health and happiness to not only Heidi but the chronically ill Clara as well.

Heidi is one of the best-known works of Swiss literature, and has spawned many film, television, and theater adaptations. One of the earliest of the movies, in 1937, starred American child-star Shirley Temple in the title role. Switzerland even has a theme part named Heidiland which is a favorite tourist attract, particularly with Japanese and Korean visitors.

*Technically, Pippi is not an orphan, yet she is a child who lives on her own without parents.

In 2015, the Swiss live action short film *Parvaneh* (2012) by Iranian-born Swiss director Talkhon Hamzavi, was nominated for an Academy Award. The film tells the story of a young Afghan immigrant living in a center for asylum seekers in the Swiss mountains, who has to travel to Zurich when her father becomes ill.

INTERNET LINKS

www.swissinfo.ch/eng/going-cuckoo-about-real-swiss-cuckoo-clocks/681210
"Going cuckoo about real Swiss cuckoo clocks" is a page on the SWI Swiss info site.

www.swissworld.org/en/culture
"One nation, diverse voices and diverse cultures" on the Swissworld site is an overview of arts and culture with links to more in-depth articles.

www.swissinfo.ch/eng/culture
The Swissinfo Culture section has articles about the latest arts and culture news.

www.myswitzerland.com/en-us/yodeling-it-s-all-in-the-voice.html
"Yodeling—it's all in the voice" is an introduction to the Swiss form of yodeling.

www.swissinfo.ch/html/swissalpinemusic/eng/index9f80.html
"Swiss Alpine Music" on this site includes a section on yodeling, as well as alphorn, and other alpine music traditions.

www.swissinfo.ch/html/swissalpinemusic/ger/swissinfo8b5f.html
This page, though not in English, has links on the right to excellent examples of yodeling.

LEISURE

A camper sits by the Stellisee (Lake Stelli) and admires the Matterhorn in the distance.

11

SURELY NOT EVERYONE IN Switzerland skis, but many do; and to be Swiss, it probably helps to be a fan of winter and mountain sports. Skiing is one of the most widely enjoyed winter activities of Swiss citizens, who seldom have to travel far to enjoy the sport. The mountains also provide bob-sledding, tobogganing, mountain hiking, and climbing.

Like most Europeans, however, the Swiss also love a sport which is neither winter nor mountain oriented. That of course is soccer, or what Europeans call football. The national team is widely supported and has participated in seven FIFA World Cups, most recently in 2014 (at this writing). Ice hockey is also a huge favorite. The Swiss National League A, with twelve teams, is, as of 2015, the most-attended European ice hockey league. Hockey is also a popular amateur sport, and most towns with a rink have a team.

SKIING

Skiing is a major tourist attraction in Switzerland and the number of places to ski and the varieties of skiing available are many. The most popular area is probably the Bernese Alps, where experienced skiers can reach the slopes of the Eiger, Mönch, Jungfrau, and Wetterhorn

Many fans regard Swiss tennis pro Roger Federer (b. 1981) the greatest male tennis player of all time. At the end of the 2014 season, he had won eighty-four Association of Tennis Professionals (ATP) singles titles including a record seventeen grand slams. Martina Hingis (b. 1980) is one of the sport's top women players.

Two girls prepare to ski the slopes in the Swiss Alps.

mountains. Scattered throughout the region are huts with cooking facilities and bunks where skiers can rest overnight as part of a long skiing trip. A mountain railway carries skiers and their equipment into the area and makes the farthest peaks accessible. In winter, after the first snowfalls and the danger of avalanches recedes, train stations are crowded with whole families setting out for a weekend of skiing.

Another region with limitless scope for climbing, ski races, or leisurely travel on skis is the Valais in the southwestern part of the country. High slopes in the region include the Matterhorn, one of the best-known mountains in Switzerland. Snow lies in this area all year round, and it is a popular place with the Swiss.

Skiing can be as expensive or as economical a hobby as each person cares to make it. Places like Saint-Moritz and Davos attract world-famous celebrities, and a stay at some of the resorts there is very expensive. The cost of buying all the latest equipment, as well as the cost of lessons, can be high.

An equally popular and less expensive form of skiing is *langlaufing* (LAHNG-loy-fink), the Swiss name for cross-country skiing. The trails are freely available to all, eliminating the high resort fees. Every year in March, thousands of skiing enthusiasts gather in the Engadine region of Switzerland for the Engadine Ski Marathon, a 26-mile (42-km) course that stretches from Maloja, past the Engadine lakes, to Zuoz. In addition to the thirteen thousand people who take part, many thousands more line the course to watch the competition.

Summer skiing is another popular leisure activity in Switzerland, although, strictly speaking, this is not snow skiing but glacier skiing. The ski routes travel along the Swiss glaciers that keep their top layer of snow all year round. The activity is usually confined to the early part of the day, since the glacier surface begins to melt by about lunchtime.

Some interesting variations have been developed on the basic theme of sliding along on skis. One sport is skijoring, where the skier is pulled along on skis by dogs, a horse, a snowmobile, or other motorized vehicle. Daredevils who love extreme sports enjoy ski hang gliding, in which the glider takes off with skis on his or her feet and uses the skis to assist in landing.

TOBOGGANING

This is a sport that developed in the late nineteenth century. The first toboggan run in Switzerland was created in 1885 by a group of vacationers from England. They tramped back and forth on a slope to compact the snow. Then they used buckets to carry snow to build the banks. The slope was ready after nine weeks of hard work.

In its early stages, the toboggan was a wooden sled with iron strips fixed to the bottom, and the riders sat upright as they slid down the makeshift runs. Later the toboggans began to take on a more aerodynamic design, and the riders learned they could achieve greater speed by lying flat. By the early twentieth century, tobogganers were achieving speeds of 60 miles per hour (97 km per hour), and resorts were building complicated toboggan runs in order to attract an influx of people who had heard about the new sport. The 1928 Winter Olympics were held in Saint-Moritz, and the toboggan run became one of the events.

Today, the most famous toboggan run is the Cresta Run at Saint-Moritz. The run consists of a series of hairpin bends along a steep ice channel. The run is about three quarters of a mile (1,212 m) in length with a drop of 514 feet (157 m). Riders can reach a speed of 80 miles per hour (130 km per hour). The Cresta Run is built from scratch every year and is open from December to February.

Old-fashioned wooden sleds are still fun for winter outdoor recreation.

Curling is a popular ice sport.

CURLING

This winter sport is played by two teams of four players who each slide two curling stones on ice toward a target. A stone is rounded on the bottom so it moves easily on ice, has handles of different colors for opposing teams, weighs 40 pounds (15 kg) and is 12 inches (30 cm) across and 4 to 5 inches (10 to 13 cm) high.

The target, called a house, is a 12-foot (3.5-m) circle with a smaller circle at its center. The object is to get the stones as close to the center as possible, and scoring is based on the position of the sixteen stones after all the players have had their turn. Each player has two throws alternating with a player from the opposing team. The player's skill lies in the way he or she gets the stone to follow a curved path. Team players smooth the stone's trajectory by using a broom to sweep the ice in front of the stone as it travels. Curling made its debut in the Winter Olympics in 1998, and Switzerland won the men's gold medal that year.

OTHER WINTER SPORTS

Ice-skating is another popular sport in Switzerland. There are many ice-skating rinks in the country, along with naturally occurring lakes where skating is practiced. Professionally, Swiss figure skater Stéphane Lambiel (b. 1985) is a national and international champ. He was the flag bearer for Switzerland at the 2010 Winter Olympics in Vancouver. Shortly after the Games ended, he announced his retirement from competition.

SUMMER ACTIVITIES

Although Switzerland's fame is as a winter sports haven, the Swiss take part in many other sports. For instance, there are many international tennis tournaments throughout summer, attended by world-famous tennis stars. Much of Switzerland's territory is made up of lakes, and there are many different watersports available for enthusiasts. Hiking and cycling are also frequent activities.

TRADITIONAL FOLK SPORTS

In addition to the internationally recognized sports that are popular in Switzerland, there are also some local sports that still make their appearance at many Swiss festivals. Swiss wrestling, or *Schwingen* is an old, rural tradition, especially in the German-speaking areas. It takes place in a circular pit and has its own special rules. The two wrestlers wear short linen, leather, sackcloth, or cotton shorts over their everyday pants. The two men grasp each other's torso, with the object of lifting their opponent off the ground, the first man to do so winning the match. Matches often attract as many as three hundred contestants and a few thousand spectators.

Two competitors take the starting hold during a Swiss wrestling match at the Festival of Alpine Horns in Nendaz.

At the Paleo Festival in Nyon, fans cheer at a concert by the British band The Cure.

Swiss farmer's tennis, or *hornussen*, is played on a large field with long wooden bats and a wooden disc instead of a ball. The fielders have to catch the disk with wooden rackets. Another traditional Swiss game is *Steinstossen*, or stone-putting. This sport dates back to ancient times in the alpine region. A player lifts a heavy egg-shaped stone over his head and throws it as far as possible. The sport requires enormous strength.

Rifle shooting and gymnastics are two popular pastimes. Around one-third of the male population of Switzerland is involved in one of these two activities. Restaurants and cafés often display trophies garnered from local shooting or gymnastics events.

A local game in Switzerland played by children is *schlagball* (SHLAG-bawhl). This game is popular in the canton of Thurgau. It is similar to American softball. There is no pitcher or catcher; the batter throws the ball up and hits it before running around the bases. Another game played by Swiss children is similar to team dodge ball. Two teams face each other across a rectangular field and attempt to eliminate the other team's players by hitting them with the ball.

OTHER PURSUITS

The Swiss workday is one of the longest in Europe, and to balance this off, the Swiss indulge in their leisure activities with relish. These include traditional activities such as folk dancing, yodeling, Alpenhorn playing, and attending concerts and the theater.

The Swiss are essentially a home-loving people. Evening activities in Switzerland tend to end early. The last movie screening begins around 8 p.m., and many parts of most cities are still and quiet by midnight. For many people, relaxing means sitting in a café with a newspaper and a glass of wine or beer, and perhaps a plate of ham or sausage. All the cafés supply newspapers, and newspapers are often found piled on street corners next to a coin box for the honest customers to drop in their money.

Much of Swiss social life revolves around the family. Friends and family often get together at one another's homes rather than go out to eat. Concerts are very popular, and many Swiss people take an active part in summer performances that feature folk singing. There are many choral societies, and yodeling clubs exist where men practice the Alpine art of yodeling, raising the voice suddenly from one pitch to another. Whereas in other countries traditional costumes, dances, and singing exist primarily for the tourists, the Swiss have a genuine interest in these aspects of their heritage and their festivals are not merely tourist-oriented.

INTERNET LINKS

www.swissworld.org/en/leisure
The Swiss government-sponsored website, Swissworld, has a section on leisure activities.

www.myswitzerland.com/en-us/swiss-wrestling-schwingen-from-herdsman-s-pastime-to-elite-sport.html
"Swiss Wrestling (Schwingen)—From herdsman's pastime to elite sport" is a look at this traditional Swiss sport.

www.myswitzerland.com/en-us/hornussen-where-the-nouss-flies-from-the-ramp-and-into-the-playing-field.html
"Hornussen—Where the Nouss flies from the ramp and into the playing field" is an article about this little known sport.

www.stmoritz.ch/en/winter/activities/ice-sports/cresta.html
This St. Moritz site includes info about the Cresta Run and other winter sports.

FESTIVALS

An "Evil Spirit" adds color to the International Alpine Horn Festival in Nendaz, Switzerland.

12

THERE ARE MORE THAN A HUNDRED different festivals celebrated in Switzerland. The large number isn't necessarily because the Swiss are exceptionally festive—though perhaps they are—but rather because some special days are observed only in certain cantons or language regions.

It can be difficult to distinguish religious festivals from folk festivals since they are so interconnected. Many have their origin in pagan rituals much older than Christianity. This can be seen in the rituals, which include driving away evil spirits, seeking blessings for the harvest, or driving away the last of winter. But of course Christian holidays are of foremost importance, since Switzerland is a primarily Christian country.

One of the more unusual spectacles in Switzerland is White Turf, a February event in the alpine resort town of St Moritz. Horses and jockeys from around the globe race across the frozen Lake of St. Moritz for big prize money. In one kind of race, called or skijoring, horses pull men on skis at high speeds.

Horses pull skiers in a fast-paced skijoring race in St. Mortiz.

In addition, as with any nation, the Swiss celebrate their own history. In 1991 Switzerland celebrated its seven-hundredth anniversary as a confederation. Four years previously, people in several of the central cantons voted against any spectacular displays since these would be environmentally harmful and extravagant. As a result, the year-long celebrations were marked by small festivals in each village, with displays of traditional Swiss skills such as yodeling and flugelhorn playing, exhibitions, and concerts rather than any huge centralized displays or celebrations.

WINTER IN SWITZERLAND

New Year's Day, January 1, kicks off the calendar year of festivities. The following day is called Berchtold Day in some cantons and is celebrated with parades. In Hallwil, in the canton of Aargau, folks come out for the colorful spectacle of the *Bärzeli*, a parade of costumed figures symbolizing concepts like fertility, age, ugliness, wisdom, and vice. This concept gets a somewhat different treatment in Urnäsch, where *silvesterklause* ("spirits of the new year") go from house to house to wish families a prosperous year. Participants in traditional costume wear cowbells, masks, and glowing headgear that are often huge and illustrate scenes from rural life.

In mid January in the Engadine, unmarried boys and girls in traditional costume travel in decorated sleds from one village to another. In Basel, the Vogel Gryff ("Griffin") festival celebrates community ties, depicted by three symbolic figures: the wild man of the woods, a lion, and a griffin (a mythical lion with eagle's head). Accompanied by mummers, or merrymakers dressed in masks and strange costumes, the three figures dance and parade in the streets. The characters are traditional symbols of three societies in the northern part of the city called Kleinbasel. In earlier days, they served military and political purposes, but now the festivities are simply a very old tradition in the district. There are many vibrant local events like this one throughout Switzerland.

The next event in the Christian calendar is Lent, a time when Switzerland abounds with festivals, the origins of most of which are completely lost. In villages around Lötschental, people dress up in hideous masks and goatskins, carry cowbells, and run around the villages making a lot of noise to scare away all the evil spirits. Other areas celebrate their own versions of this event.

In Luzern, Zürich, Bern, and especially Basel, six weeks before Easter, tens of thousands of masked or brightly costumed celebrants take part in Fasnacht, a three-day carnival similar to the New Orleans' Mardi Gras. The dramatic and colorful festival begins at 4 a.m. when all the lights in the city are turned off. Piccolos and drums then start playing in the pitch dark. Lanterns are lit, providing the only light until daybreak approaches. The masks and elaborate costumes that participants wear add to the carnival spirit. The festival continues for three days with decorated floats and more pipe-and-drum bands.

A colorful parade in Basel revives a centuries-old tradition of masked and costumed performances or Fasnacht.

SWISS SPRING

Holy Week is the high point of the religious spring calendar. On Maundy Thursday, the eve of Good Friday, Christ's washing of His disciples' feet is celebrated in Catholic communities. In Fribourg, the bishop, as a token of humility, kisses the feet of the faithful in the cathedral. On Good Friday there are many religious processions in the towns of southern Switzerland. In Mendrisio, a passion play, or reenactment of Christ's final hours, is performed on Maundy Thursday and Good Friday. Easter Sunday is celebrated much as it is throughout Christian Europe, with church, family feasts, decorated eggs, and chocolate. In Switzerland, however, the cuckoo brings the Easter eggs, and chocolate cuckoos may take the place of chocolate bunnies.

May Day is an important folk event all over Europe, and in Switzerland many small villages hold festivals. In Geneva two children, a boy and a girl, are named the May King and Queen. They are solemnly crowned on the

The annual spring parade of guilds in Zurich celebrates the end of winter (even in the rain).

second Sunday of May and lead a procession from house to house through their home village.

On Ascension Day, thirty-nine days after Easter, Lucerne observes a ceremony dating to 1509. Priests carry the holy sacrament around the village on horseback, blessing the crops. For Corpus Christi, three weeks later, streets in Appenzell are strewn with carpets of flowers. In Kippel, the Grenadiers of God march through the town in nineteenth-century uniforms to commemorate the event. In Romont, in western Switzerland, part of the procession is a group of shrouded weeping women carrying representations of Christ's shroud, crown of thorns, and other things associated with the crucifixion.

SUMMER CELEBRATIONS

June sees the return of the cows to the high pastures in regions such as the Valais, Gruyère, and Appenzell, and this event is marked by many festivities. The men who herd the animals dress in traditional costume and decorate their cows with flowers and bells. There are flag-tossing competitions, Alpenhorn playing, traditional dances, and Swiss wrestling. In the lower Valais, there are cow fights in which cows are rarely harmed, but the winning cow becomes queen of the herd and wears an enormous cowbell.

Throughout the summer, Tellspiele is a grand theatrical event in Interlaken. The story of William Tell is retold in Johann Schiller's eighteenth-century play, *Wilhelm Tell*, with a cast of more than two hundred performers and live animals.

Flower-bedecked cows wear giant cowbells on their descent from the high pastures in a late summer festival.

Every July, the town of Sempach celebrates the Battle of Sempach in 1386, when a small Swiss force was able to defeat Duke Leopold III of Austria. National costume is worn and the armor of the time is dusted off for the festivities.

Swiss National Day, August 1, celebrates the meeting in the field at Rütli, where the first Swiss cantons forged a defensive alliance in 1291. The day is celebrated with readings of the federal pact, torchlight processions, fireworks, and bonfires throughout the country.

AUTUMN TIMES

Fall brings harvest festivals throughout the rural regions of Switzerland. These are accompanied by flower processions, especially in Geneva, Lugano, and Neuchâtel.

Knabenschiessen is a three-day shooting contest in September in Zurich. About five thousand girls and boys ages thirteen to seventeen compete to win the coveted title *Schützenkönig,* or "king of marksmen." The event includes a folk festival of fairs, rides, and food stands. September also sees the observance of a federal Thanksgiving Day, which does not involve turkey

but rather is meant as a fasting day of prayer.

November 1 is All Saint's Day, a day to honor the dead. People may visit the graves of their ancestors, light candles, or attend church services. In December Geneva celebrates the Escalade, which remembers the day in 1602 when the Duke of Savoy tried to conquer the city using ladders to scale the city walls.

In the Klausjagen, men wear ornate paper headdresses, which are lit from inside by candles.

The coming holiday season is marked with Christmas markets which feature seasonal foods and crafts. These markets, which take place in all the big cities, are great tourist attractions.

CHRISTMAS

In common with other European countries, Switzerland's Christmas festivities begin on December 6, when the feast of Saint Nicholas is celebrated. The tradition of giving gifts, which takes place on Christmas Eve, began with this saint's day. Saint Nicholas is the patron saint of youth, and gifts are given in honor of his generosity.

In Küssnacht, a village on the north shore of Lake Lucerne, the *Klausjagen* ("Nicholas chase") is an old tradition. In the procession through the streets at night, participants wear huge hats, or bishop's miters, illuminated from the inside. At the end of the parade is St. Nicholas himself, attended by four companions called *Schmutzlis* who hand out pastries. Festivities carry on through the night, with people celebrating in bars and wandering the streets cracking whips, blowing horns, and ringing bells.

SAMICHLAUS AND SCHMUTZLI

Delivering Christmas gifts to the good children of the world must be a difficult job, because Santa doesn't work alone. In the United States, he has elves to help him out, but in Europe, Santa's assistants appear in a number of guises.

First off, the European Saint Nick is more of a Father Christmas figure than an American-style Santa Claus. He wears the bishop's robes of his fourth-century Saint Nicholas forebear and can be more solemn. In the German part of Switzerland, Saint Nick, or Samichlaus, is accompanied by a strange-looking figure called Schmutzli (from schmutz, meaning "dirt"). He is a frightening character with a concealed or blacked-out face and red eyes.

In the French part of Switzerland, this attendant is called Père Fouttard, or Father Fouttard, from the French fouet, or "whip." Sure enough, like Schmutzli, he often carries a stick or switches with which he threatens children against misbehavior.

In another Swiss Christmas tradition, carolers form a singing Christmas tree in Zurich.

This scary Christmas figure has numerous counterparts in other European countries, all with slightly different characteristics. He goes by the name of Zwarte Piet ("Black Peter") in Holland; Hans Trapp in the Alsace-Lorraine section of France; the Krampus, or "Christmas Devil," in Austria, Bavaria, and Slovenia. The character has other incarnations as well.

These days, Schmutzli and his cousins are fairly benign figures who look scary but don't really hurt anyone. In the old days, however, they were much more likely to put their switches to use on any child they deemed to be naughty.

MANY KINDS OF FESTIVALS

Switzerland has many festivals dedicated to art and music. In 1938 Toscanini began a music festival in Lucerne, and each year world-famous orchestras and conductors come to the city to perform in the concert hall by the lake. Zürich has a music festival where the emphasis is on opera, and Montreux and Gstaad also have classical music festivals, and the Montreux Jazz Festival in early July is world famous.

Zürich also holds a jazz festival and an arts festival in June, with all the arts represented. There are concerts, art exhibitions, operas, and plays in all the national languages, as well as folk music, street theater, and music. Geneva's *Fête de la musique* ("Music Festival") includes classical orchestras, electro jazz bands, rock, pop, world music, and French music. Other music festivals include every imaginable type of music—blues, jazz, soul, funk, hip-hop, reggae, world music and more.

Would it be Switzerland without a yodeling festival? In June, the Eidgenössisches Jodelfest brings together about fifteen thousand yodelers every three years for competitions and performances.

FOOD FESTIVALS

Harvest is an occasion for festivals that celebrate the year's crops. In the wine-growing areas, there are many wine festivals. The one at Vevey is unusual as it is celebrated rarely—only five times in the twentieth century. The festival dates back to the Middle Ages when there was a winemaker's guild. This guild awarded prizes to the best workers in the vineyards, who then paraded through the town. By the seventeenth century, the event had become a celebration of the wine god, Bacchus, with the god himself portrayed in the procession by a small boy seated on a barrel. Ceres, a goddess, was also represented, along with other figures from mythology.

More recent festivals have added fife and drum bands from Basel and herdsmen from Gruyère. The last festival was in 1999 and was a very elaborate affair. Planning began six years before, and the festival involved around five thousand people and hundreds of goats, oxen, and horses.

In the Bernese Alps, a new festival has been created by an old tradition. It was, and still is, common for the farmers of the region to pool their milk in order to make cheese. Once the cheese is ready at the end of summer, it is given out to each farmer in proportion to the milk produced by his cows. Once upon a time it may have been a simple operation, but today it has been turned into an event, with stalls selling the cheese and lots of wine and food served to the accompaniment of music.

Bern is also the home of the Onion Festival, or *Zibelemärit*, which take place in November. Onion tarts, soups, quiches, sausages are available, as well as wreaths and folk arts made of braided onions. Cheeses, breads, and mulled wines round out the experience.

Onions are made into dolls at the Onion Market in Bern.

INTERNET LINKS

www.timeanddate.com/holidays/switzerland
Time and Date has a calendar of Swiss holidays with links to explanations.

www.swissinfo.ch/eng/culture/schmutzli--the-swiss-santa-s-sinister-sidekick/7082046
This article explains the Swiss Christmas character Schmutzli.

www.expatica.com/ch/about/Swiss-festivals_106810.html
Top Festivals in Switzerland 2015 is a long list of fun events. Check for updates in later years.

FOOD

Wheels of cheese rest on shelves at a factory.

13

SWISS COOKING IS AS VARIED AS THE kinds of the people that make up the country. It is an interesting mix of French, German, and Italian cooking with some distinctively Swiss dishes thrown in. Staples vary from area to area, but potatoes are popular everywhere. In the Italian-speaking Ticino area, rice is the staple, while polenta, a dish made from corn, is also popular. Switzerland is of course famous for its cheeses. It produces its own wine and many forms of dried and cured meat. The best known Swiss dish is fondue, a dish of melted cheese and wine served with bread.

In Switzerland, there is no cheese called "Swiss cheese." That's an American name for cheese that resembles the Swiss hole-filled cheese Emmentaler. Another Swiss cheese, Gruyere, also has holes.

REGIONAL DISHES

Regionally, the cuisines of Switzerland follow the linguistic makeup of the country. In western Switzerland, cooking styles have French influence. Northern Italian dishes predominate in the south, while the rest of the country tends to favor German cuisine. In the west, fish dishes are the speciality. Bernese salmon or many of the freshwater fish such as char, grayling, and trout are simply cooked in butter. Mushrooms are also important in western Swiss cooking, and mushroom sauce is used for a variety of dishes, such as the highly popular *Züricher geschnetzeltes* (TSUE-rish-err guh-SCNETTS-ell-tess). The west also specializes in cured pork.

In Lucerne, Zug, and other parts of central Switzerland, a popular regional dish is cheese soup. A Zürich speciality is a meat stew made from strips of meat and served with the German version of *rösti*, or pan-roasted potatoes. *Ratsherrentopf* (rahts-HAIR-un-topf) is another Zürich dish made from several different stewed meats and potatoes.

In the Valais and Graubünden, dried meats are expensive and much in demand. The meat is hung in the arid air of the mountain slopes and left to dry out completely. It is not smoked. The meat is sliced very thinly and served with pickled onions or gherkins as an hors d'oeuvre.

In Bern and the Rhine cantons, veal is popular and often cooked in cream sauce and served with noodles. Another speciality is *mistkratzerli* (MIST-krahts-err-lee), a dish of a small young chicken served with baked potatoes. Saint Gall and Basel are famous for their own variety of sausage.

An *assiette Valaisanne* is a platter of meats and gherkins.

A NATION OF CHOCOLATE LOVERS

Although cocoa beans don't grow in Switzerland, the Swiss have played a major role in the development of chocolate. Today the country is a top producer with a reputation for the highest quality chocolate. Many well-known brands are native to Switzerland, including Lindt, Nestle, and Toblerone.

In 1819, François-Louis Cailler opened the first chocolate factory in Switzerland after studying chocolate-making in Italy. He developed a way to turn gritty chocolate into a smooth product that could be made into bars. But chocolate at this point was still mainly used in drinks. In 1879, Swiss chocolate-maker Rodolphe Lindt improved upon the process by adding cocoa butter and inventing a rolling and stirring machine called a conche. This advancement greatly improved the taste, texture, and melting quality of chocolate. That same year, Lindt's countryman, Daniel Peter, came up with the idea of adding powdered milk to chocolate to create milk chocolate. Henri Nestle, another Swiss, began by manufacturing milk products. He worked so closely with Daniel Peter, however, that he eventually went into the chocolate business.

Other Swiss folks who played important roles in the history of chocolate-making include Phillippe suchard, Jacques Foulquier, Charles-Amédée Kohler, Rodophe Sprüngli-Ammann, and Jean Tobler, who created the Toblerone bar in the late 1860s.

In 2014, the Swiss ate more than 19 pounds (9 kg) of chocolate per person, making Switzerland the top chocolate-consuming nation in the world. (For comparison, Americans that same year ate about 9.7 pounds (4.3 kg) per person.)

MÜESLI, THE ORIGINAL SWISS GRANOLA

In 1900, a Swiss physician created a dish for the patients in his clinic in Zürich. Dr. Maximilian Bircher-Benner(1867–1939) believed in a diet rich in fresh fruits, nuts, and raw vegetables. His approach to nutrition was quite at odds with the thinking of the day, which emphasized meat and bread. Bircher-Benner also stressed strict physical exercise and an early-to-bed, early-to-rise daily schedule. He based his theories on the lifestyle of shepherds in the Swiss Alps.

The dish he is famous for became known as müesli; in Switzerland, where it's still very popular, it's called Birchermüesli. The doctor's original recipe was a combination of uncooked rolled oats, grated apple, chopped hazelnuts or almonds, soaked in a little cream and lemon juice and eaten with plain yogurt.

Today, packaged müesli can be easily found in the cereal aisle of most grocery stores. It may contain other rolled grains, such as wheat, rye, or corn flakes, along with dried fruits, nuts, and seeds. Some versions are sweetened with honey and spiced with cinnamon. The difference between müesli and granola, which is a similar cereal dish, is that the oats and other grains are raw in müesli; in granola they are baked until crispy.

Ticino is famous for its rice and noodles, as one would expect of an Italian-speaking region. *Busecca* (boo-seck-ka), a soup made from tripe, and a dish of snails served with walnuts are also Ticino specialities.

CAKES AND PASTRIES

The most popular cakes in Switzerland are called *leckerli* (LEKK-err-lee), which are flat and oblong-shaped spiced honey cakes topped with a coating of sugar icing. They vary from place to place, being made with bear-shaped candies on the top in Bern. *Gugelhupf* (goo-gell-HOPEF) is another regional cake that is popular all over Switzerland. It is a large bun with a hollow center that is often filled with whipped cream. *Birnenbrot* (BEER-nenn-brote) is a teabread made with dried fruit, while *fladen* (FLAH-den) and *krapfen* (KRAHP-fen) are richer fruit cakes filled with nuts, almond paste, and pears. *Kirschtorte* (KIRSH-torta), a cherry tart from Zug, has become another national favorite. From the Engadine comes *nusstorte* (NOOSE-tore-ta), a tart made with a walnut caramel filling.

This *gugelhupf* is glazed, but the cake can also be sprinkled with powdered sugar or filled with whipped cream.

THE POTATO

It is not only the Irish who have made great use of the potato. Arriving in Switzerland sometime in the seventeenth century, the potato soon became a very important part of the Swiss diet. The Swiss have devised many delicious ways of preparing the humble potato.

In Swiss cooking, potatoes are rarely served plain or even as French fries. They are cooked whole in their skins or boiled, and then pureed, piped on

to baking trays, and baked to make potatoes au gratin, or they are boiled, diced, dried, and then pan-fried to make *rösti*. Potatoes are also an important element of the cheese dish *raclette* (rah-KLEHT), in which melted cheese is poured over boiled potatoes, cornichons (tiny gherkins), pickled onions, and sometimes slices of dried meat, such as ham or sausage.

SWISS CHEESE

Swiss cheese is famous because of Emmentaler, the cheese with the large round holes running through it. But there are many types of Swiss cheeses other than this one type.

Emmentaler has its holes because of the way it is made. Over the four months that the cheese is left to ferment, it produces carbon dioxide that forms into bubbles, and as the cheese sets, the bubbles become fixed within it. Regularly shaped and perfectly round bubbles are a sign that the cheese has fermented properly. The cheese originated in the thirteenth century in Emmental Valley, in the canton of Bern.

Gruyère is another very famous Swiss cheese. Others are not so widely known. *Tête de Moine* is a soft cheese made in a cone-shaped block from which the cheese is scraped. *Vacherin*, a cream cheese made in the Jura, is stored in round boxes made from birchbark. It ripens during the summer and is ready by November.

Raclette is a dish made from melted Swiss cheeses, mostly *bagnes* (BAHH-nyeh) and *conches* (kahnch) cheeses made in the Valais. The cheeses are cut in half and left by an open fire to melt. When they are ready, they are poured over potatoes boiled in their skins and served with pickled spring onions and gherkins. Other popular cheese dishes are *croûtes au fromage* (KROOT oh frahm-MAZH)(cheese toasts), cheese quiche, and cheesecake.

Traditional cheese fondue is a Swiss mountain favorite.

FONDUE

The cantons of Valais, Vaud, and Geneva all claim to have originated this famous Swiss dish. The cheese is melted in a pot, which is brought to the table and kept at a bubbling temperature over a flame. Diners each have a plate of chunks of white bread that they spear on a long, two-pronged fork and dunk into the sauce. As the sauce boils away, it gets stronger and better. Traditionally, the person who lets bread fall into the pot has to buy a bottle of white wine for all the diners. One way to avoid this is to choose a cube of bread with crust on it. Tea and dry white wine are traditionally served with the fondue.

Today, packaged fondue cheese mixes can be purchased and simply emptied into a pot to melt. Other versions of fondue include recipes using other cheeses, and dessert fondues made of melted chocolate.

SWISS WINES

Swiss wines are not as famous as French or German wines and are rarely found outside of the country. This is because they are in such great demand in Switzerland itself that the supply does not cover the foreign demand.

People in the west and south of the country consume more wine than people in the German-speaking areas, who consume more beer. It is thought that the grapevine was first brought to Switzerland by the Romans. Grapevine cultivation in the country, however, picked up only in the twelfth century. The Swiss make mostly white wine in the Valais, Vaud, and Neuchâtel regions, where the long dry summers favor wine growing. Ticino grows mostly black grapes that make the red wines.

A 1993 statute regulates the production of both ordinary and premium wines, while alcohol in general is regulated by the Constitution. Sixteen-year-olds can legally purchase wine and beer in Switzerland, but need to wait until they are eighteen to buy spirits and other forms of alcohol.

A vineyard in the Lavaux region

A CULINARY CALENDAR

Many traditional Swiss dishes are linked to special times of the year. At New Year, the traditional dish in Ticino is *zampone* (zam-POHN-nee), stuffed pig's feet cooked with lentils, while in Graubünden, smoked pork with vegetables in barley soup is eaten.

Shrove Tuesday brings deep fried crisp wafers of pastry. In the canton of Ticino, whole villages bring out huge pots in which they cook risotto, stirring it constantly with enormous wooden spoons. It's served with garlic-flavored pork sausages.

At Easter, the traditional dish is lamb or kid, and it is customary for families to go off to the country-side to pick dandelion greens for their salads.

In the fall, when the shooting season starts, chamois, a kind of mountain goat, is on the menu.

Before the use of feed grain made it possible to keep animals alive through winter, huge amounts of meat became available in the markets in the fall, and smoked and cured meats still abound during this period.

One dish common at this time in Switzerland is *bernerplatte* (BAIR-nair-PLAHT-ta), which consists of cured and smoked meats served with potatoes and sauerkraut or French green beans.

A butcher sells his meats at a farmers' market in Grindelwald.

INTERNET LINKS

www.myswitzerland.com/en-us/typical-food.html
This page offers a nice overview of Swiss favorites by region.

allrecipes.com/recipes/world-cuisine/european/swiss
This site is a good bet for Swiss recipes using American measures

www.info-galaxy.com/Chocolate/History/Swiss_Pioneers/swiss_pioneers.html
"Swiss Pioneers" is a section in this history of chocolate.

CROÛTES SUISSE (SWISS TOASTS)

Also called *croûtes au fromage* (cheese toasts), this can be made with or without the wine. Alternatively, in lieu of wine, you could use cider.

For each serving:

1—2 slices of crusty, country-
style bread (*pain de campagne*),
thickly sliced

1—2 garlic cloves

light sprinkle of nutmeg (optional)

white wine (Savoie wine is
traditional, but any crisp, light
white will do; or cider)

Swiss cheese: Emmentaler,
Gruyere, or Raclette

Preheat oven to 425°F.

Butter a baking dish big enough to hold all bread slices in one layer. Lightly toast the slices of bread. Rub each slice with a cut garlic clove. Then, dip the toasts into a shallow dish of wine. If desired, sprinkle toasts lightly with nutmeg. Cover with thick slices of cheese. Bake until cheese is melted and bubbly.

Serve with pickled onions and cornichons (tiny French gherkins).

Variations: The Swiss often add ham and tomatoes to their croûtes. The French like to add bacon. Another option is lightly sautéed onions. Add whatever you like on top of the wine-soaked bread and then top with the cheese. If you wish, top with a fried egg after the croûtes come out of the oven.

ÄLPLERMAGRONEN (SWISS MAC AND CHEESE)

This Alpine farmer's dish is served topped with onion rings and warm apple sauce.

2 large waxy potatoes, peeled and cut into
   1-inch cubes
1 lb macaroni or penne pasta
2 large onions, peeled and sliced
4 Tbsp butter
3 cups grated cheese (Raclette, Gruyere,
   Emmentaler, or Appenzeller)
2 cups milk, cream, or half and half
applesauce

Heat oven to 375°F.

Boil a large pot of salted water.

Heat the butter or oil over medium-low heat in a frying pan. Add onions and fry them until golden brown. Add pasta and potatoes to the salted water. Cook until tender, stirring occasionally, about 15 minutes. Drain.

Heat the milk or cream until hot but not boiling, and add salt and pepper.

In an oven-proof casserole dish, place one-third of the pasta and potatoes, and sprinkle with half of the grated cheese. Make another layer the same way, and top with the remaining pasta and potatoes. Pour the seasoned milk or cream evenly over the top.

Cover with the browned onions.

Bake covered for 15 to 20 minutes until steaming hot and cheese is melted. Serve with warmed applesauce.

MAP OF SWITZERLAND

ECONOMIC SWITZERLAND

Manufacturing

- Chemicals
- Chocolates
- Electrical Appliances
- Machinery Manufacturing
- Pharmaceuticals

- Precision Instruments
- Textiles
- Watchmaking

Services

- Banking & Finance
- Tourism

Agriculture

- Grapes
- Livestock
- Olives
- Tobacco
- Vegetables

ABOUT THE ECONOMY

OVERVIEW

Switzerland is a peaceful, prosperous, and modern market economy with low unemployment, a highly skilled labor force, and a per capita GDP among the highest in the world. Switzerland's economy benefits from a highly developed service sector, led by financial services, and a manufacturing industry that specializes in high-technology, knowledge-based production. Its economic and political stability, transparent legal system, exceptional infrastructure, efficient capital markets, and low corporate tax rates also make Switzerland one of the world's most competitive economies.

CURRENCY

1 Swiss franc (CHF) = 100 centimes
USD1 = CHF 0.95 (April 2015)
CHF1 = $1.05
Notes: 10, 20, 50, 100, 200, 500, 1000
Coins: 5, 10, 20 centimes; 1/2, 1, 2, 5 francs
(Since 2002 the euro is also accepted in Switzerland.)

INFLATION RATE

0.4 percent (2015)

GROSS DOMESTIC PRODUCT

$371.2 billion (2013)

GDP SECTORS

Agriculture 0.7 percent, industry 26.8 percent, services, 72.5 percent (2013)

LAND AREA

15,938 square miles (41,290 sq km)

AGRICULTURAL PRODUCTS

Eggs, fruit, grains, meat, vegetables

INDUSTRIES

Machinery, chemicals, tourism, textiles, watches, precision instruments, banking, insurance

EXPORTS

Machinery, chemicals, metals, watches, agricultural products

IMPORTS

Machinery, chemicals, metals, motor vehicles, textiles, oil, natural gas, agricultural products

TRADE PARTNERS

Germany, United States, Italy, France, Netherlands, United Kingdom, Austria

AIRPORTS

International airports: Zürich, Geneva, Basel Regional airports: Bern-Belp, Saint Gallen, Lugano-Agno.

LABOR FORCE

5 million (2013)

UNEMPLOYMENT RATE

3.2 percent (2013)

CULTURAL SWITZERLAND

Basel
This town boasts one of Switzerland's finest city gates, the Spalentor, which was constructed in the late fourteenth century as part of the town's fortification efforts. Basel is home of a medieval cathedral, which has red sandstone walls, two slender towers, and a colorful roof. The town also has an imposing City Hall, which was built from 1507–1513.

Zurich Old Town
Especially appealing in Zurich Old Town are the three landmark churches: the Fraumünster, Grossmünster, and St. Peter's Church, all of which are more than 800 years old. The Grossmünster's unique twin spires are a distinct Zurich landmark. The tower clock of St. Peter's church has Europe's largest clock face with a diameter of 29 feet (8.7 m).

Benedictine Abbey of Einsiedeln
This abbey is a stunningly beautiful example of baroque architectural skills, considered by many to be Switzerland's most beautiful church building. A pilgrimage site since the Middle Ages, the newly restored abbey features the Lady Chapel with the Black Madonna.

Bern
Not only is Bern the capital of Switzerland, it also houses many interesting museums, historical arcades, and lovely old architecture. In 1191 Duke Berthold V of Zähringen named the city after the first animal—a bear—he killed in a hunt. Living bears have been kept as the city's pets since 1513. Even today there are bear pits in the center of the town.

Tell Museum
This museum in Bürglen, which is the birthplace of William Tell, contains a large collection of documents and articles of both historical and artistic character from over six centuries. The quaint, well-preserved Tell village, now part of the museum, is guarded by a tower.

Lucerne
Lucerne has breathtaking scenery and numerous medieval structures, such as the two covered bridges, Kapellbrücke (Chapel Bridge) and Spreuerbrücke (Spreuer Bridge), which span across the Reuss River. Both bridges are adorned with beautiful paintings and one even has a small chapel, built in 1568, in the middle.

Montreux Jazz Festival
This is one of the world's most respected jazz festivals and has been held every summer in the beautiful lakeside town of Montreux since 1966. Its offerings also include other styles of popular music, such as rock and rhythm and blues.

Castle of Chillon
Erected in the thirteenth century in Montreux, near Lake Geneva, this castle was originally a fortress but underwent many transformations over the next centuries. It was also used as a residence for the Counts of Savoy and as a state prison. The castle was made famous by Lord Byron, who wrote a poem titled "The Prisoner of Chillon" in 1816.

The Matterhorn
Though not the highest peak in Switzerland, the Matterhorn is still one of the most frequently climbed mountains in the world. Apart from mountain climbers, it attracts tourists with its unique beauty. The Matterhorn has a sharp, isolated rock pyramid with steep narrow ridges jutting from surrounding glaciers. The town of Zermatt, nestled at the foot of the mountain's northern face, became a major tourist resort mainly because of the Matterhorn.

Swiss Transportation Museum
This highly visited museum in Lucerne has all kinds of vehicles on display, such as steam and electric locomotives, railroad cars, automobiles, engines, horse-drawn coaches, bicycles, an old postal coach, antique and modern airplanes, space capsules, and aerial cable railways. It even has a space suit that was worn on the moon and lake steamers dating as far back as 1813.

ABOUT THE CULTURE

OFFICIAL NAME
Confederaziun Helvetica, or Swiss Confederation

NATIONAL FLAG
A red field with a bold, equilateral white cross in the middle that does not extend all the way to the edges of the flag.

NATIONAL ANTHEM
Schweizer Psalm (Swiss Psalm). The music and lyrics were written by Alberich Zwyssig and Leonhard Widmer, respectively. It was adopted as the national anthem in 1961.

CAPITAL
Bern

OTHER MAJOR CITIES
Zürich, Geneva, Basel

ADMINISTRATIVE REGIONS
26 cantons

POPULATION
8,239,600—including 1,937,400 foreign nationals (2015)

POPULATION GROWTH RATE
0.78 percent (2014)

MEDIAN AGE
42 years (2014)

LIFE EXPECTANCY AT BIRTH
82.4 years (2014)

ETHNIC GROUPS
German 65 percent, French 18 percent, Italian 10 percent, Romansh 1 percent, other 6 percent

LITERACY RATE
99 percent (2014)

OFFICIAL LANGUAGES
German, French, Italian, Romansh

NATIONAL HOLIDAYS
New Year's Day; Epiphany (January 6); Good Friday and Easter Monday (March/April); Labor Day (May 1); Swiss National Day (August 1); Assumption (August 15); All Saints' Day (November 1); Christmas Eve; Christmas Day; New Year's Eve

LEADERS IN THE ARTS
Arthur Honegger (composer), Bruno Ganz (actor), Paul Klee (painter), Sophie Taeuber-Arp (painter), Conrad Witz (painter), Arnold Böcklin (painter), Ferdinand Hodler (painter), Alberto Giacometti (painter and sculptor), Max Frisch (writer), Adolf Muschg (writer), Denis de Rougemont (writer), Johanna Spyri (writer)

TIMELINE

IN SWITZERLAND	IN THE WORLD
20,000 BCE–4,000 BCE Neanderthals populate Neuchâtel.	
Fifth–first centuries BCE Celts establish La Tène civilization.	**753 BCE** Rome is founded.
58 BCE Julius Caesar defeats Helvetii Celts and establishes a long period of Roman rule over much of present-day Switzerland.	**116–117 BCE** The Roman Empire reaches its greatest extent, under Emperor Trajan.
400 CE Germanic people move into Switzerland after the Roman Empire's collapse.	**600 CE** Height of Mayan civilization
Fifth–first centuries CE Switzerland comes under control of the Franks and later becomes part of Charlemagne's Holy Roman Empire.	**1000** The Chinese perfect gunpowder and begin to use it in warfare.
1291 Three cantons sign a common defense treaty and found the Swiss Confederation.	**1530** Beginning of transatlantic slave trade organized by the Portuguese in Africa
	1558–1603 Reign of Elizabeth I of England
	1620 Pilgrims sail the *Mayflower* to America.
	1776 US Declaration of Independence signed.
1797–1798 Under Napoleon Bonaparte, French forces invade Switzerland and replace the Confederation with the Helvetic Republic.	**1789–99** The French Revolution
1815 After Napoleon's defeat, the Congress of Vienna restores the former Swiss Confederation and recognizes Swiss armed neutrality as a permanent policy.	
1850 Rapid industrialization makes Switzerland the second most industrialized country in Europe after Great Britain.	**1861** US Civil War begins.

IN SWITZERLAND	IN THE WORLD
	1869 The Suez Canal is opened.
1914–18 Switzerland remains neutral in World War I.	**1914** World War I begins.
1939–45 Switzerland is neutral in World War II but strikes accommodations with both sides.	**1939** World War II begins.
	1945 World War II ends.
	1949 The North Atlantic Treaty Organization (NATO) is formed.
	1957 The Russians launch *Sputnik*.
1959 A coalition government of four parties takes and remains in power until the present.	**1966–69** The Chinese Cultural Revolution
1971 Swiss women get the right to vote.	
	1986 Nuclear power disaster at Chernobyl in Ukraine
	1991 Breakup of the Soviet Union
	1997 Hong Kong is returned to China.
1999 Switzerland gets its first woman president, Ruth Dreifuss.	
2002 Switzerland joins the United Nations.	**2001** Terrorists crash planes in New York, Washington, DC, and Pennsylvania.
	2003 War in Iraq
	2011 Earthquake and tsunami devastate Japan
2014 Swiss voters reject proposal to limit immigration.	
2015 Switzerland hosts international nuclear negotiations with Iran.	**2015** German pilot deliberately crashes plane into the French Alps, killing 150.

GLOSSARY

Alpenhorn
Long, powerful horn of wood or bark used chiefly by Swiss herdsmen for communicating in the Alps.

Corpus Christi (KORH-puhs KRIS-tee)
Roman Catholic festival in honor of the Eucharist or Holy Communion.

fondue (fahn-doo)
A popular Swiss dish of melted cheese, usually flavored with white wine and kirsch, a cherry liqueur, and eaten with bread.

hornussen **(horh-NOOS-ehn)**
Often called farmer's tennis, this traditional Swiss sport has a vague similarity to American baseball.

Landsgemeinde (LAHNTS-geh-min-de)
The outdoor parliament held in spring when citizens vote for their representatives.

polenta (poh-LEHN-tah)
A kind of gruel made from cornmeal.

predestination
A Calvinist belief that a soul's eventual destiny, especially its place in heaven or hell, is foreordained by God.

raclette (rah-KLEHT)
Melted cheese served with potatoes.

Romansh (roh-MANCH)
Language spoken primarily in eastern Switzerland.

rösti **(ROHRS-tee)**
Pan-roasted potatoes.

schlagball **(SHLAG-bawhl)**
Game similar to American softball.

skijoring
Skiing while being pulled along by a horse or by vehicles, such as a jeep.

Sonderbund
Separatist league formed on December 11, 1845, by seven Catholic Swiss cantons to oppose anti-Catholic measures by Protestant liberal cantons. The term Sonderbund also refers to the civil war that resulted from this conflict.

yodel
To sing by suddenly changing from a natural voice to a falsetto and back.

FOR FURTHER INFORMATION

BOOKS

Bewes, Diccon. *Swiss Watching: Inside the Land of Milk and Money*. Boston: Nicholas Brealey Publishing, 2012.

Czupryn, Adriana et al., *DK Eyewitness Travel Guide: Switzerland*. New York: DK Publishing, 2013.

Nelson, Kay Shaw. *Cuisines of the Alps*. New York: Hippocrene Books, 2005.

Spyri, Johanna. *Heidi*. New York: Puffin in Bloom, 1880, 2014.

Steinberg, Jonathan. *Why Switzerland?* Second edition. Cambridge, U.K.: Cambridge University Press, second edition, 1996.

VIDEOS

Switzerland's Amazing Train Rides, Questar Video, 2014, DVD.

Zermat, Switzerland—Under the Shadow of the Matterhorn, Travelscope, LLC., 2013.

WEBSITES

CIA World Factbook, Switzerland www.cia.gov/library/publications/the-world-factbook/geos/sz.html

Frommer's Switzerland www.frommers.com/destinations/switzerland

The Local www.thelocal.ch

My Switzerland.com www.myswitzerland.com

Swissworld.org www.swissinfo.ch/eng

BIBLIOGRAPHY

Bojanowski, Axel. "Land O' Lakes: Melting Glaciers Transform Alpine Landscape." Spiegel Online International, April 26, 2013. www.spiegel.de/international/europe/melting-glaciers-turning-alps-into-lake-region-a-896729.html

Bosley, Catherine. "Swiss End to Bank Secrecy One Step Closer as Law Revamp Proposed." Bloomberg, Jan. 14, 2015. www.bloomberg.com/news/articles/2015-01-14/swiss-end-to-bank-secrecy-one-step-closer-as-law-revamp-proposed

CIA World Factbook, Switzerland www.cia.gov/library/publications/the-world-factbook/geos/sz.html

Cohen, Roger. "The (Not So) Neutrals of World War II." *The New York Times,* Jan. 26, 1997.

The Economist, "Don't Ask, Won't Tell." Feb 11, 2012. www.economist.com/node/21547229

Erlanger, Simon. "Is There a Future for Jews in Switzerland?" Jerusalem Center for Public Affairs, March 15, 2007. jcpa.org/article/is-there-a-future-for-jews-in-switzerland

Expatica, "Swissworld: Religion in Switzerland" www.expatica.com/ch/insider-views/Swissworld-Religion-in-Switzerland_107839.html

Gregoire, Carolyn. "Why Switzerland Has Some of the Happiest, Healthiest Citizens in the World," *The Huffington Post,* Oct. 7, 2013. www.huffingtonpost.com/2013/10/07/switzerland_0_n_4038031.html

The Local, "Celebrated Swiss artist Erni dies at age 106." March 22, 2015. www.thelocal.ch/20150322/celebrated-swiss-painter-dies-at-age-106

Misicka, Susan. "One in four shuns religion in Switzerland." Swissinfo.ch, March 31, 2011. www.swissinfo.ch/eng/empty-pews_one-in-four-shuns-religion-in-switzerland/29877728

Morgan, Victoria. "Being Swiss gives contemporary artists a leg up." Swissinfo.ch (SWI), June 10, 2012. www.swissinfo.ch/eng/being-swiss-gives-contemporary-artists-a-leg-up/32813996

My Switzerland.com www.myswitzerland.com

Porter, Darwin and Danforth Prince. *Frommer's Switzerland,* 15th edition. Hobokken, NJ: John Wiley & Sons, 2012.

Revill, John, and Andrew Morse. "Calls to Curb Muslim Immigration Rise in Switzerland." *The Wall Street Journal*, Jan. 12, 2015.

"The Swiss Confederation: A Brief Guide 2015" Federal Chancellery www.bk.admin.ch/dokumentation/02070/index.html?lang=en

Swissworld.org www.swissinfo.ch/eng

Steinberg, Jonathan. *Why Switzerland?* 2nd ed. Cambridge, England: Cambridge University Press, 1996.

Timeanddate.com "Holidays in Switzerland 2015." www.timeanddate.com/holidays/switzerland

Wernick, Robert. "In Search of William Tell." *Smithsonian Magazine*, August 2004. www.smithsonianmag.com/history/in-search-of-william-tell-2198511/?no-ist

INDEX

INDEX